POSITIVELY INTROVERTED

Finding Your Way in a World Full of People

by Maureen "Marzi" Wilson

ADAMS MEDIA

NEW YORK   LONDON   TORONTO   SYDNEY   NEW DELHI

for Kiko and Mochi,

who love me

(and barely tolerate each other)

Adams media

Adams Media
An Imprint of Simon & Schuster, Inc.
100 Technology Center Drive
Stoughton, Massachusetts 02072

First Adams Media hardcover edition April 2022

ADAMS MEDIA and colophon are trademarks of Simon & Schuster.

For information about special discounts for bulk purchases, please contact Simon & Schuster Special Sales at 1-866-506-1949 or business@simonandschuster.com.

The Simon & Schuster Speakers Bureau can bring authors to your live event. For more information or to book an event contact the Simon & Schuster Speakers Bureau at 1-866-248-3049 or visit our website at www.simonspeakers.com.

Interior design by Colleen Cunningham
Illustrations by Maureen Wilson

Manufactured in China

10 9 8 7 6 5 4 3 2 1

Library of Congress Cataloging-in-Publication Data
Names: Wilson, Maureen (Cartoonist), author.
Title: Positively introverted / by Maureen "Marzi" Wilson.
Description: Stoughton, Massachusetts: Adams Media, 2022.
Identifiers: LCCN 2021043839 | ISBN 9781507216682 (hc) | ISBN 9781507216699 (ebook)
Subjects: LCSH: Introverts. | Self-help techniques.
Classification: LCC BF698.35.I59 W55 2022 | DDC 155.2/32--dc23/eng/20211007
LC record available at https://lccn.loc.gov/2021043839

ISBN 978-1-5072-1668-2
ISBN 978-1-5072-1669-9 (ebook)

TABLE OF CONTENTS

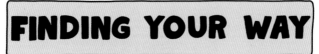

INTRODUCTION

Hi, I'm Marzi! I'm an introvert...but I didn't always know that. I spent most of my life thinking I was really weird because I liked being alone more than I enjoyed socializing. (I've since realized I am actually a *little bit* weird, but that's unrelated to my introversion.)

When I finally discovered I was an introvert, I spent a lot of time researching temperament and exploring how it influenced daily life. I learned a great deal about what it means to be an introvert, but I didn't really know what to *do* with that information. If you're an introvert, too, you might feel the same confusion.

After all, we introverts live in a world designed for extroverts. To be healthy and happy, we need to figure out how to navigate within the world.

Easier said than done, right? From relationship disasters to friendship struggles to workplace snafus, I was encountering an endless series of challenges that undermined my introversion. To overcome these obstacles, I realized I needed to be proactive about protecting and nurturing my quiet nature.

HARD

QUESTIONS

After years of trial and error (and lots of therapy!), I've had enough experiences—both positive and negative—to fill a book....So here we are! We're going to figure out how to approach the world on our own (introverted) terms. Whether that means setting clear boundaries, carving out some precious "alone time," or talking through your feelings, this book is full of ideas on how to embrace your introverted nature. Pour a cup of tea, find a quiet spot, and curl up with your coziest blanket, because we have a lot to talk about....

embarrassing stories

POSITIVELY INTROVERTED
how to find your way in a world full of people

portable

edible

affirming

(not really, but that would be cool!)

Chapter One	# THE INS AND OUTS OF INTROVERSION

If you picked up this book, you were likely drawn to it because you're an introvert (or suspect you might be). Hooray! It's always wonderful to meet another introvert (from a distance, that is).

In this chapter, we'll get started with the basics. We'll talk about the ins and outs of introversion: how introverts differ from extroverts, the particular needs and challenges of introverts, and what sort of gifts introverts have to offer the world.

Maybe you already feel pretty certain that you're an introvert. Or perhaps you aren't quite sure. Luckily for you, I've created a list of "Top 10 Signs You're an Introvert." How many of the following describe you?

~the~ FINE PRINT

Not all of the items on this list will apply to every introvert. After all, we're unique individuals!

1. You refrain from sharing your ideas until you've had time to think things through. You feel flustered or irritated when others demand an immediate response.

2 You feel most at peace when you're alone. Solitude brings you serenity, and you enjoy your own company. As I like to say, "often alone, rarely lonely."

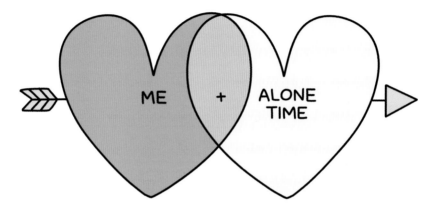

3 You crave quiet, cozy spaces; crowded locations make you feel tense. Parties are overwhelming! You'd much rather be on the sidelines than in the thick of the festivities. When celebrations get too chaotic, you have a habit of disappearing.

4 You have a heightened sensitivity to stimuli. Loud sounds startle you, while extended exposure to noise often results in a headache. You find bright lights especially bothersome.

5 You thoroughly consider potential outcomes and consequences when making decisions. You're uncomfortable with unnecessary risk-taking, especially when the stakes are high.

6 You have one or two best friends rather than a large group of buddies. While others say "the more the merrier," you say "the fewer the better." You prefer to invest your energy in deep, close relationships instead of spreading yourself thin. You're extremely loyal to the few who are a part of your inner sanctum.

FRIENDSHIP PYRAMID

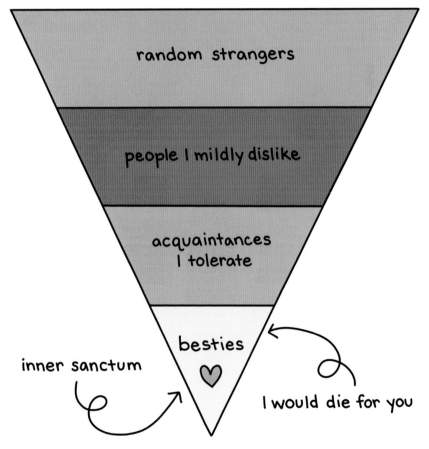

random strangers

people I mildly dislike

acquaintances
I tolerate

besties

inner sanctum

I would die for you

7 Your home is your sanctuary. You've cultivated a space that suits you, and there are few places you'd rather be. When you have a choice between staying in or going out, you almost always want to stay home. If there's an unexpected knock on the door, it feels like an intrusion of your personal space. You wish people would text before dropping by!

8 You find social interactions emotionally and physically draining. Even if you're participating in an activity you enjoy, with people you like, there is a limit to how much you can handle. When you push yourself beyond that limit, you feel frazzled and on edge. You tend to excuse yourself early and head home long before everyone else.

9 You spend a lot of time thinking. Then thinking some more! Your brain is a vibrant place, and there's always something new to ponder. Maybe you like to "build" things in your head. Or perhaps you have a fantasy world you escape to? You find it a bit odd when other people complain that they're bored….How could anyone be bored when there are so many possibilities to imagine?!

10 You feel somehow different, as though you don't meet society's standard of "normal." People often ask, "Why are you so quiet? Are you mad? Is something wrong?" After a while, you begin to wonder the same thing: *Is there something wrong with me?*

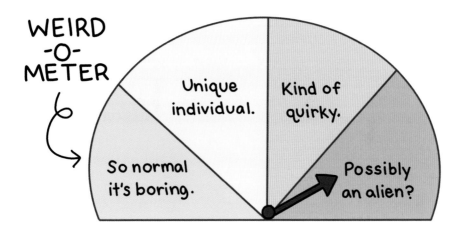

Did several of those sound familiar? If so, you're likely an introvert. Welcome to the club!

In essence, being an introvert means that you feel drained by interactions with others, and you "refuel" by being alone. Conversely, extroverts typically feel energized by socializing with people. Of course, introverts are capable of socializing (and even enjoy it, on occasion). And extroverts won't perish if they have to spend an evening at home. But your natural temperament—introversion or extroversion, or somewhere in between—shapes your particular preferences and needs.

Introvert Fuel

Solo activities help introverts "refuel"!

Treat yourself!

"CAT TREATS" cereal

Fortified with A, B, C, D, etc.

Juicy!

Just add milk!

PAPERBACK SnACKS

Check it out!

Now with more cuddles!

Movie Munchies

Cheesy!

Addictive!

Yummy!

I didn't always know that I was an introvert; I certainly didn't understand my own reclusive tendencies. Why did I feel so alone in a crowd? Why did I dread events everyone else seemed to enjoy? Why was I such a party pooper?

I *wanted* to want to socialize...but when Friday night rolled around, all I *really* wanted was to be cozy in bed with a book. On my better days, I simply thought I was boring. On my worst days, I felt broken.

When it finally (FINALLY!) dawned on me that I was an introvert, I was at last able to see myself with unclouded clarity. There was a word for people like me, and it wasn't "party pooper." It was "introvert"!

That realization shed light on my formative childhood experiences, while illuminating some challenges that puzzled me well into adulthood.

introvert problems

It was a long time before I connected the dots and figured out that many of my daily struggles were fundamentally "introvert problems." I wish I'd known sooner that I wasn't the only one dealing with those issues; it would have been so validating to know that others experienced similar difficulties. I'm going to briefly touch on some of those challenges here, because I want you to know what I did not: *You are not alone.*

It's important to note that although we may encounter problems due to introversion, that doesn't mean we are the *cause* of those problems. Many complications arise simply because we are living in a world with extroverted expectations—and we certainly can't be blamed for that!

Don't feel discouraged by this section!

This book was written precisely to help introverts navigate tricky issues.

We'll explore solutions in the following chapters.

One problem area for introverts is the issue of miscommunication. Many extroverts are unaware that introverts process information differently, and that means we *communicate* differently.

...so now you understand why I reacted that way, right?

Huh?

Mm-hmm.

doesn't seem to get it

seems to get it

While extroverts may fire off rapid assertions in a disagreement, introverts are more likely to pause and think before responding. I've had frustrating incidents where my reaction was misinterpreted; others assumed I was disengaged or being stubborn. I've frequently had to scramble to explain my behavior to people who just didn't seem to "get" it.

Further misunderstandings arise when we need to distance ourselves because we're desperate for downtime. Have you ever had friends or family misinterpret your (very legitimate) request for alone time? Some people view this desire for solitude as a personal rejection; they can't fathom why we would want to seclude ourselves to recharge.

Alone time is essential for our mental and physical well-being. Introverts simply need space...a lot of it!

Another thing that many extroverts have a hard time understanding: Even when introverts are visiting a "fun" place, it isn't fun for long—unless we can take frequent breaks to maintain our equilibrium. It's difficult for introverts to tolerate the onslaught of sound and the glare of bright lights for an extended period of time.

"Fun" places that aren't fun for long:

amusement parks

concerts

public pools

Introverts need frequent breaks while in crowded, noisy spaces.

You've likely faced most—if not all—of those troublesome issues. Perhaps, like me, those introvert problems have led you to some big questions.

BIG QUESTIONS TO PONDER

Is there room for me?

What do you call a cold hot dog?

Where do I belong?

What do I have to offer?

Is it legal to be named Anonymous?

You might be wondering if there's a place for introverts on this crowded planet. Where do we fit in? Is there room for our reserved and quiet ways? Do we have anything of value to offer?

Posing those questions can feel a bit disheartening. "Marzi," you say, "this has been a gloomy chapter! I thought this book was supposed to help me feel better about being an introvert, not worse!"

Uh-oh, did you buy the wrong book? Better double-check the cover!

Guaranteed to make you feel worse!

NEGATIVELY

Now with 100% more gloom!

Devastation INTROVERTED

POSITIVELY

Cute doodles

Helpful advice!

INTROVERTED Validation

Whew! Looks like you got the right one.

Don't stop reading now! I assure you, we deserve to be here as much as anyone, and introversion comes with numerous gifts the world urgently needs.

For example, introverts are independent thinkers who don't need to be micromanaged. Since we work independently, we form ideas that are unexpectedly original. The inherently thoughtful nature of introverts sparks novel solutions to complex problems.

This is our home, too!

24

That introvert originality means we also have a talent for creating. Many introverts have careers that involve writing, designing, building, or coding. Our brains think outside the box, and creativity is one of our most powerful assets.

In addition to our beautiful brains, our bodies are unique because our senses are, well, extra sensitive. I mentioned how that can sometimes be an obstacle, but it can also be an advantage. Our heightened awareness comes in handy when we observe small details others might miss. We perceive even the slightest shift in our surroundings; that seems like an evolutionary advantage, don't you think?

Many introverts are sensitive to noise and easily pick up on sounds others might not. (Hey, it isn't my fault that I overheard my parents' private conversations!)

Introverts are not only gifted at hearing; they are also skilled at *listening*. Have you noticed how silence makes most extroverts uncomfortable? They rush to fill the silence when we're quiet— and we're often quiet. So, when it comes to listening, I guess you could say that we've had a lot of practice. We have an aptitude for distilling rambling narratives into simpler concepts. Our observant nature + our proclivity for deep thinking = remarkably perceptive interpretations.

My mother-in-law is sooo sweet, she gave me a brand-new vacuum! She said mine must not work very well. Also, she made me this sweater... I usually wear yellow, but she said this color looks better on me. Her bunions are bothering her, bless her heart, so she's going to stay with us and put her feet up until she feels better.

I sense you're feeling resentful, but it would rock the boat if you set firm boundaries.

OMG are you a mind reader? Are you PSYCHIC?!

Discovering and embracing my introversion was a major step forward in terms of my personal growth. My inner awareness was expanding, but I was unsure how to apply that knowledge in a practical sense.

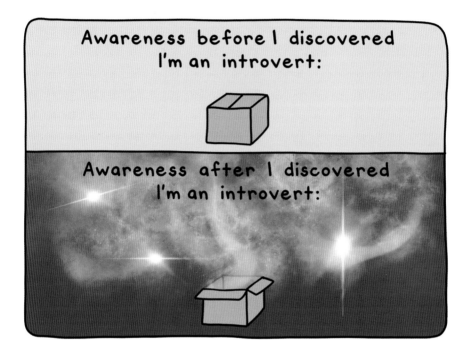

I was an introvert in a world designed for extroverts, and I still needed to figure out how to find my way in a world full of people. Acknowledging my introversion was only the starting point in that long journey.

<table>
<tr>
<td>Chapter Two</td>
<td>

IT STARTS WITH SELF

</td>
</tr>
</table>

After exploring the ins and outs of introversion, I felt ready to discover how I could utilize my introvert strengths to thrive in this crowded world. As I contemplated where to start, I reached the conclusion that my well-being depended on my willingness to look backward and turn inward.

In this chapter, we'll contemplate how the early life experiences of little introverts can shape self-perception well into adulthood. We will first reexamine the messages absorbed in childhood, and then work to reframe them in a healthier way.

It's time to take a look at who you once were, and how that has impacted who you are today. As you look backward, you can begin to move forward...

I can recall a distressing incident when I felt confused and lost. As panic began to overwhelm me, I remembered my mother's instructions: "When you're lost, look for an adult and ask for help." Unfortunately, that occasion was last week, and I had to remind myself that I *am* an adult.

When I was younger, I envisioned the progression to adulthood as a linear path forward. I'd begin as a child, grow into a teenager, and finally emerge as a fully formed, all-knowing adult. I've since decided that was a naive expectation.

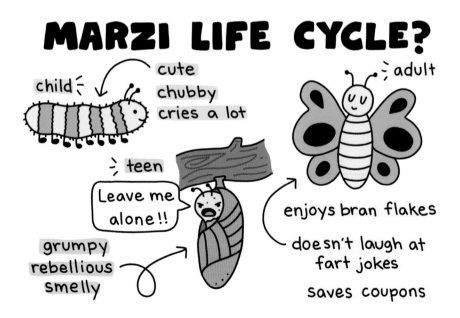

30

To my dismay, I did not become an adept adult the moment I blew out the candles on my eighteenth birthday cake. I mean, yes, I was *technically* an adult. And these days, I do manage to accomplish some adult-y things with regularity (more or less). But there are still times when I feel much like I did at age sixteen, twelve, or six. I sometimes have an adolescent urge to rebel, resisting rational, grown-up behavior. At other times, I feel overwhelmed and small, longing for a responsible adult to help me find my way.

I found that becoming an adult was less about *moving on* to the next stage of life, and more about *building upon* all the stages that came before. Those younger versions of me—Marzi at age six, twelve, sixteen, etc.—they still exist, in some sense. I carry the experiences of my childhood with me, and they've helped shape who I am today.

SOME THINGS I HAVEN'T OUTGROWN

	frequent napping	missing mommy	acting cranky in public	thinking denim vests are cool
child	yep	sniffles	TANTRUM	needs glitter
teen	always	rolls eyes	stomps	with patches
adult	...zzz	yeah	sighs	it has pockets!

What does that have to do with the introvert journey? It's true that being an introvert is about temperament and innate traits...but being a grounded, healthy introvert is also about developing a strong sense of self. In order to do that, you must first look backward to scrutinize those early events that helped shape who you are. Then you must look inward to discern how those experiences align with your current knowledge of introversion.

Turning inward is what I do best!

Many of the negative messages absorbed in childhood continue to smolder beneath the surface, unexamined and unchallenged. "Marzi," you say, "is that really such a big deal? After all, those things happened a very long time ago. And now I am a mature adult who pours milk into a glass instead of drinking straight from the carton." As I've learned (the hard way), the stuff rumbling below the surface has a way of bubbling up in unexpected ways at inconvenient times. That can get messy!

Uh... I don't drink from the carton, either.

Eh, this old thing? It's been around for ages. I'm not worried about it.

bullying shame criticism judgment rejection insults

I internalized negative messages about introversion more than I realized, and they influenced my day-to-day life for years to come. How many of these judgmental statements sound familiar?

As a child, I accepted others' harsh opinions of me as fact, even though it hurt to do so. Were they right in thinking there was something wrong with me? Was I broken? I believed their words, and I carried those beliefs into adulthood.

I can still recall some unpleasant encounters of my youth with sharp focus. I can visualize where I was, who was speaking to me, and how their words made me feel. I relive the hot flush of shame that made my cheeks burn, and the helplessness of not knowing how to react.

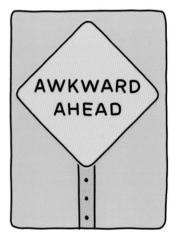

I'm going to share an embarrassing experience I had in grade school. In retrospect, the story is a bit silly, but I feel it highlights the challenges introverted kids often encounter.

My teacher, Mrs. Delaney (name changed 'cause legal stuff), was a forceful, no-nonsense woman with a booming voice and a huge presence. After one parent-teacher conference, my mom mentioned how Mrs. Delaney complained that I "jumped a foot" whenever she spoke to me. That wasn't much of an exaggeration; as a quiet little introvert, I found her terrifying.

One fateful day, I was finishing my school lunch in the cafeteria when Mrs. Delaney came to fetch me. She stood in the doorway and bellowed my name, then turned sharply to storm down the hall. I could hear someone say, "Ooo she's in *trouble*!" It felt like everyone was staring as I scrambled to follow her.

In my panic to leave the lunchroom, I didn't realize I was still clutching my wrapped ice cream sandwich. As we passed the bathroom, I tried to quickly duck inside to throw it away.

Mrs. Delaney always warned, "I have eyes in the back of my head," which was apparently true. Without turning around, she snapped, "Don't you dare try to hide in that bathroom!"

illicit ice cream sandwich

Well, now I had a bit of a problem.
It was against the rules to take food from the cafeteria, and I wasn't able to dispose of the ice cream without Mrs. Delaney noticing. So I did the only thing I could: I discreetly slid the ice cream sandwich into my sock.

Makes Total Sense

"Marzi," you say, "was that *really* the only thing you could do?"

OTHER THINGS MARZI COULD HAVE DONE

dropped it

shared it

eaten it

Okay. Maybe it wasn't the *only* thing I could have done. But it was the only thing I *thought* to do. In any case, I now had an ice cream sandwich nestled against my ankle.

When we arrived at the classroom, Mrs. Delaney yelled at me for leaving pencil shavings beneath my desk.

crime scene

I hung my head to avoid her intense gaze, but this angered her further. "Look at me when I am speaking to you!" she shouted. "What do you have to say for yourself?"

You can probably guess what I said: nothing. The pressure of the confrontation was too great, and I couldn't string my thoughts together into a sentence. "Are you *ignoring* me?" Mrs. Delaney spluttered.

Then the inevitable happened. The ice cream sandwich began to melt, soaking through my sock. It pooled inside my shoe and dripped on the floor, forming a gooey puddle.

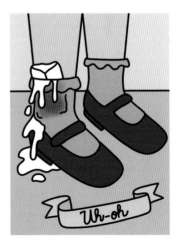

Mrs. Delaney went deathly quiet. Mrs. Delaney was never quiet. Now, as a little introvert, I normally liked silence. But I did not like this, not at all. Mrs. Delaney slowly leaned forward until her face was inches from mine, and delivered what I thought was a life sentence: "I am *keeping* you, and you will help the custodian *clean the school*," she hissed. "You will *not* be going home on the bus."

The bell rang, and as the other students streamed into the classroom, I sat down stiffly at my desk. My face was fiery, my ankle cold and sticky. Mrs. Delaney said she was *keeping* me and I *wouldn't be going home*. I would be held captive as the custodian's assistant, forever scrubbing the school like a modern-day Cinderella. I tried to hold back tears as I thought about how I would never see my parents again.

I remember sobbing that afternoon as I scrubbed the classroom floor on my hands and knees while the custodian uncomfortably looked on. At some point, my mother was called, and she came to rescue me.

As I revisit that memory with the knowledge I now have about introversion, I'm struck by a few aspects of that encounter:

1 Mrs. Delaney called me out in a public way, making me the center of attention while my classmates stared. Most introverts are uncomfortable being in the spotlight, and respond better when they are quietly taken aside. Had Mrs. Delaney done that, I might not have panicked and taken the ice cream with me.

2 When I tried to throw away my ice cream sandwich, Mrs. Delaney misinterpreted my intentions and presumed the worst. It's natural for introverts to want to solve a problem without asking for others' input or permission. Since we don't see the need to offer an explanation, people can be cynical about our motives.

3 Introverts tend to be deep thinkers, but not necessarily hasty thinkers. Without time to consider my options, I made the unfortunate decision to wear an ice cream sandwich. Not a good look.

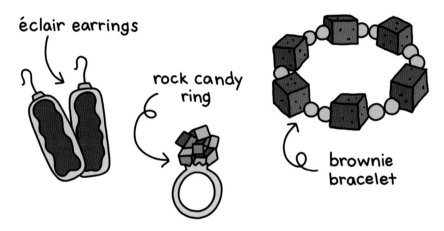

éclair earrings

rock candy ring

brownie bracelet

4 Mrs. Delaney's approach wasn't a productive way to handle conflict with an introvert. Yelling, aggressive demands for eye contact, and ignoring the boundaries of physical personal space—introverts find these gestures to be overwhelming and invasive.

5 Finally, there was a lack of understanding on both sides. Mrs. Delaney presumed I was ignoring her when I couldn't instantly verbalize my thoughts. In turn, I misconstrued the scope of Mrs. Delaney's punishment. Introverts have busy brains and big imaginations; when we lack concrete details, we fill in the blanks with our own ideas. It's possible to get a little carried away (and become an imprisoned princess in the process).

As I considered whether I should share that awkward experience here, I realized there are a lot of embarrassing stories I've never shared with anyone. I typically carry my humiliations alone, and then replay them while I lie sleepless at night.

I'm not implying that you need to share all of your painful experiences with the world. We are introverts, after all, and are private by nature. But there's something to be said for retelling these stories, at least to yourself.

As an adult who has a greater understanding of introversion, you can reread your stories with a fresh perspective. You have the opportunity to analyze events in a more objective way, to recognize that you weren't bad, or wrong, or broken...you were just a misunderstood, introverted kid.

Take a moment to consider the ways you internalized the criticisms you heard as a child. How have they influenced your self-perception as an introvert? Have they impacted your choices and how you navigate the world?

If you're discerning a link between past events and your current behaviors, may I suggest a strategy that helped me diminish harmful thought patterns?

Would you like to hear the strategy?

If **YES** continue reading.

If **NO** proceed to Chapter 3.

As I look back on the hurtful experiences of my youth, I find myself wondering, *Where were the supportive adults while this was happening?* Sometimes it was just a group of kids being unkind; other times it was the adults themselves who were being cruel.

In any case, I was often left to fend for myself. As I visualized little introvert Marzi feeling broken and lost, I found myself wishing I could be there for her, as a caring and accepting adult.

I allowed myself to let my introvert imagination explore that idea more fully. I envisioned my older self, advocating for my younger self.

I thought about the encouraging feedback little Marzi needed to hear. I imagined saying those words until she believed them, and as I did so, I felt the peace and affirmation that had eluded me for so long.

I spent years ignoring the shame beneath the surface, pretending my childhood experiences didn't affect me. Once I reached adulthood, I just wanted to move on. I didn't want to dig up my past to examine how those negative messages shaped me. What I didn't comprehend was that my refusal to look backward was blocking my way forward.

Whether I wanted to admit it or not, I had internalized those messages. It wasn't until my understanding of introversion deepened that my perspective of events broadened. I now had the necessary framework to reevaluate and challenge those painful encounters. As I finally looked backward and turned inward, I could see that the damaging messages were but a

small part of a wider panorama. There was much more to the story—there was much more to *me*—than I'd realized.

Although you can't change past events, you can reframe your experiences by drawing on the knowledge you've since gained about introversion. You can rewrite your personal narrative by nurturing your younger self with comfort and validation.

Once upon a time, there was a little girl named Marzi, who was both quiet and kind.

That brings me back to where this chapter started: I sometimes long for a supportive adult. And then I remember that *I can be the adult I need*. When panic and despair begin to overwhelm me, I ask myself what words I need to hear, and then I say: *There's nothing wrong with you. It's okay to do things differently. You deserve to be treated with respect. You are lovable just as you are.*

I say them until I believe.

Chapter Three

FAMILY FUNCTIONS

All families have complex, interwoven histories. These are the people who have known you the longest. You've shared memories and rivalries, inside jokes and arguments. For introverts, family dynamics can pose a unique challenge—how do you fit in and celebrate yourself in a group dynamic?

In this chapter, we'll talk about the roles we play within our families, and how our identities are often defined by others. We'll discuss ways to explain to our families who we are as introverts, then explore how to establish necessary boundaries while still enjoying everyone's company.

Let's talk about how our families function, and how we can navigate those relationships in a healthy way.

The concept of families has always struck me as somewhat odd. Adults make or adopt additional people without knowing who, exactly, those extra people will turn out to be. They live together in close quarters with minimal privacy. They eat together, travel together, and spend their weekends together. There are tears and tender moments. Drama! Comedy! Tragedy! It sounds like a riveting premise for a reality TV show, doesn't it? Oh, and did I mention it continues FOR AT LEAST EIGHTEEN SEASONS?

But when you consider that it is, in fact, reality, the concept seems more torturous than entertaining for introverts. We spend our formative years with people we wouldn't necessarily

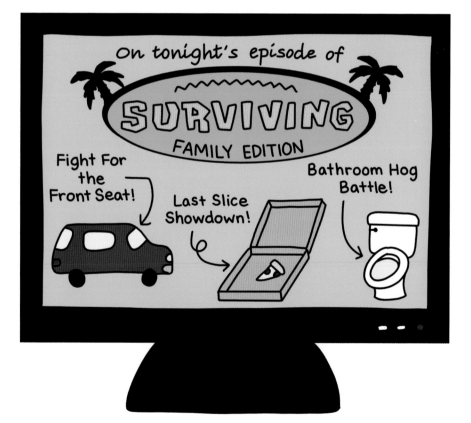

decide to live with, if given a choice. Perhaps, like me, you sometimes fantasized about living entirely on your own (or possibly with a pod of dolphins).

Since I grew up with doting parents and endearing siblings (who could blackmail me with embarrassing photos), I'll be

speaking in general terms about common family issues. (See, Mom? *General* terms…so please don't post those photos of me trick-or-treating as a baked potato.)

In early family life, roles, labels, and expectations are often quickly and

Don't be a hater, give a treat to this tater!

rigidly established. For example, the oldest child was stuck with all the responsibilities, while the youngest was spoiled. (That is, unless you happened to be the youngest...then the oldest child had all the privileges while the youngest was just sent to bed early.) I think the one thing that we can all agree on is that the middle child got lost in the shuffle. (Can you tell that I'm a middle child?)

Some of us had specific roles we were expected to fill. Maybe you had to be the responsible one, making sure chores were completed. Perhaps you felt like you had to be the person who ensured everyone got along. Were you expected to be the well-behaved, obedient child because your sibling was more than a handful?

Over time, others' expectations of us could become enmeshed with our own sense of identity. As children, it seemed as though

everyone else decided *who we were.* Did you get stuck with a childhood nickname you just couldn't shake? I did! (Yes, sometimes my family still calls me by that name. No, I'm not telling you what it is.)

It wasn't uncommon for our families to give us labels we had little say in (sometimes because we weren't old enough to talk).

For some reason, it was determined that our earliest behaviors were indisputably linked to our

future identities. Did you gnaw on a pencil as a teething tot? Bam, you were an artist! Did you pick up a ball that rolled your way? Bang, you were an athlete! Did you hide under your bed when your mom arranged a playdate? Boom, you were an antisocial weirdo!

And there's the problem. While most labels were relatively benign, there were some labels—like, for an *entirely hypothetical* example, "super-spooky-quiet kid"—that could cause harm.

Here's a story about a family label that took me years to live down. One afternoon I was playing a Scrabble game with my grandmother and brother. As a bookish, word-loving little introvert, I felt quite confident that I would win. I grew suspicious when my brother played his *third* blank tile (for you not-so-wordy introverts, there are only two blank tiles in Scrabble).

He was turning the tiles over and using them as any letter he wanted! I caught on to his sneaky scheme and accused him of cheating. My grandmother chided, "You're a poor sport, and no one likes a poor sport." Well, the prophecy was spoken, the words set in stone, and I was labeled a "poor sport" for years to come (much to my brother's glee).

On the flip side of being labeled and told who we were, we were also defined by *who we were not.* Not athletic, like your sister. Not outgoing, like your brother. Not the teacher's pet, like your cousin. When others were used as the measuring stick of your worth, you often fell short. As your family was actively defining you, it became increasingly difficult for you to define yourself.

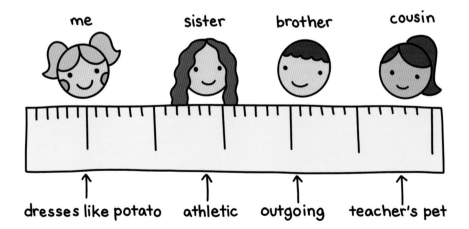

In the previous chapters, we talked about how the hurtful messages we internalized as kids could influence our self-perception as adults. When it comes to families, there's an added layer of complexity, because our relatives don't (usually) fade from our lives like grade school bullies and teachers. Chances are, there's still some contact with family members, and the messages they sent in earlier years can continue to influence our relationships with them today.

"Oh, no, Marzi," you say, "I'm not that easily influenced! I never hold a grudge. Forgive and forget!" That is an impressive creed to live by, but I'm not really talking about anything as overt as a "grudge." I suspect family dynamics are swayed by a subtler force: the force of habit.

Sometimes we continue to act in roles we never asked for, accepting labels and identities that don't reflect our true selves, because that's how things have always been. Our families have fixed perceptions and expectations that seem unlikely to change.

It might be helpful to pause for a moment to consider which of their perceptions align with our true selves.

Their Perception	My Truth
She's a nerd.	I like to learn.
She's selfish.	I take care of my needs.
She spends too much time online.	I like connecting with online friends.
She's antisocial.	I'm social on my own terms.
She's a weirdo.	I'm one-of-a-kind.
She's dramatic.	I feel things deeply.
She's a loner.	Solitude rejuvenates me.

Have you ever considered how many of their opinions stem from misconceptions about introversion? Just as you found it helpful to learn the ins and outs of introversion, your family members might also benefit from seeing the bigger picture. If you want your family to understand you better, they first need to understand *introversion* better.

It's essential to clearly explain which traits go hand in hand with an introverted temperament (refer to Chapter 1). It's difficult for others to give us what we need if they aren't made aware of those needs. I realize it can be a challenge to have conversations about introversion with family members who are very extroverted. Since they perceive the world differently, it's important to find a mutual frame of reference.

When I'm trying to explain my introvert needs to others, I find it helpful to use analogies. Here's a general one you might like to try:

You might also find it useful to think about experiences you've shared together, using that common ground as a starting point for dialogue about introversion.

So, what if you've tried your best to explain your temperament to your family, but they're still giving you a hard time about your introverted tendencies? That's where the beauty of boundaries comes in.

BEAUTIFUL boundaries

Boundaries are the invisible lines we draw between what's okay and what's unacceptable. "But Marzi," calls out a random person from the back corner, "shouldn't we be trying to compromise instead of drawing lines all willy-nilly?"

Good question, random person! Yes, being open to compromise is an important aspect of maintaining healthy relationships, and we will discuss that more in Chapter 5.

However, I'm willing to bet that you've already spent *years* attempting to compromise with relatives who have repeatedly taken advantage of your quiet, reserved nature. If you're consistently being steamrolled, firm boundaries are essential.

Although inconvenienced family members might insist otherwise, the concept of "setting boundaries" is not equivalent to "always getting your way." Boundaries are simply about protecting your well-being. They are not a hallmark of selfishness, but an indicator of self-respect.

I can recall a session with my therapist when I mentioned some extra responsibilities I'd agreed to. Although I was under a great deal of stress, I bravely pronounced, "I'm going to keep doing as much as I can, for as long as I can, until I know I can't do it anymore."

My therapist paused for a long moment, then asked whether I thought that was a good idea. Well, sure. I wanted to be helpful and kind. Wasn't contributing as much as I possibly could the right thing to do?

He gently asked, "Have you considered whether it might be wise to cut back on commitments *before* you reach the point of burnout?" No, actually, I hadn't considered that, but I've thought of his suggestion many times since.

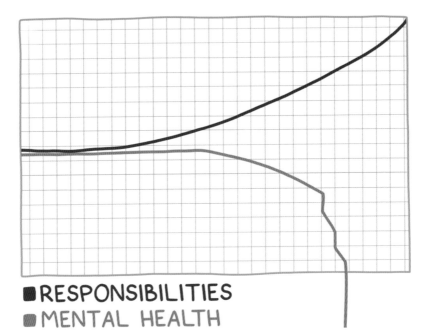

■ RESPONSIBILITIES
■ MENTAL HEALTH

Setting boundaries can be tricky for introverts, as many of us are non-confrontational. We might wish to avoid a particular topic if we fear it could lead to an argument. Plus, there's that whole "force of habit" problem we talked about earlier. We question whether certain issues are worth bringing up after all this time. However, when we consider whether something is worth addressing, we should also consider the cost of *not* addressing it. Relationships without boundaries can lead to resentment, burnout, and exploitation, which isn't healthy.

To establish boundaries, consider what you can give without sacrificing your own well-being. Here's one way to clarify your thoughts: Divide a sheet of paper into two columns. Label one "What They Want" and the other "What I Can Reasonably Give." List the demands placed on you, then consider your own needs to determine where boundary lines should be drawn.

Say, for example, that your endearing sister likes to drop by your house almost every day. She invites herself in, asks for coffee, and ends up staying for dinner. Meanwhile, your work piles up, and once she leaves, you feel so drained that you just want to go to bed.

What does your sister want? "Marzi," you say very sweetly, "she wants to spend time with you because she loves you." That may be true, but it isn't the whole truth. She also wants you to prioritize *her* desires over your own obligations.

Your sister is making unfair demands on your time, and you clearly can't afford to give her that much leeway. Now ask yourself, "What can I reasonably give?" It might not cost too much of your time or energy to schedule a weekly dinner. You could connect throughout the week by texting instead of enduring drop-in visits.

The key part of setting boundaries is being clear about what isn't working for you, then stating what you intend to do instead. It's possible (and preferable!) to do this in a manner that is both gentle and firm. You may get some pushback, but remember that those boundaries are essential for your well-being.

Perhaps you're worried that setting boundaries will strain your family relationships. But I've found that it can strengthen those connections, as it creates bonds founded on respect and authenticity.

Stepping outside of your assigned role within the family may initially be disconcerting, but I think you'll soon find that it's refreshing to choose how *you* wish to define yourself. As you embrace your identity as an introvert, you'll be able to show up for your family as the best, most genuine version of yourself.

But if all else fails...you can always decide to live with the dolphins.

<table>
<tr><td>Chapter
Four</td><td># HOW TO FRIEND
SOMEONE</td></tr>
</table>

Chapter Four | HOW TO FRIEND SOMEONE

Although we didn't get to choose the families we grew up with, we *do* get to choose our friends. That is, if we can figure out where to begin.

Making friends seemed somewhat easier as a child—share your snack, and you had decent odds of making a buddy. As adults, it's much more challenging (and sometimes awkward!) to find new friends. I think many introverts have asked themselves some version of this question: "In a world full of people, how do I find *my* people?"

In this chapter, we'll discuss "social needs" and whether solitude-loving introverts can benefit from friendships. We'll also tackle the logistics of how to meet potential friends (a bit tricky, given how we love to stay home). Finally, we'll talk about how to balance friendships with our introverted needs.

Let's kick off this chapter with an informative, extremely scientific* diagram of the Extrovert/Introvert Spectrum:

EXTROVERT / INTROVERT SPECTRUM

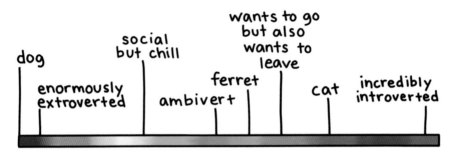

dog

social but chill

wants to go but also wants to leave

enormously extroverted

ambivert

ferret

cat

incredibly introverted

*not actually scientific

As you can see, extroversion and introversion are on a spectrum. A person can be enormously extroverted or incredibly introverted... or anywhere in between. In the middle of the spectrum, you'll find the ambiverts.

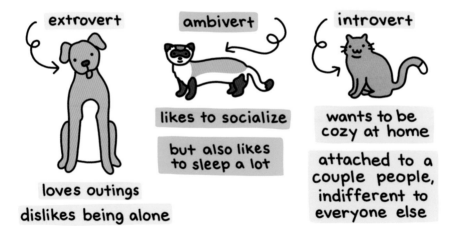

extrovert

loves outings

dislikes being alone

ambivert

likes to socialize

but also likes to sleep a lot

introvert

wants to be cozy at home

attached to a couple people, indifferent to everyone else

Ambiverts are people who are just as comfortable staying in as they are with going out. When someone asks, "Anyone wanna meet up for dinner tonight?" in a group chat, ambiverts are likely the people replying, "I could go either way."

The fine folks who reside at the introverted end of the spectrum share an overarching characteristic: They find that social interaction is draining rather than energizing. That being said, introverts can still have varying levels of "social needs." Some introverts truly enjoy going out (at first), but gradually wind down until they can escape. Other introverts have very little desire to wander any farther than the mailbox. Let's zoom in at our highly scientific* diagram for a closer look:

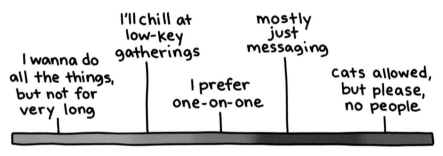

INTROVERT SOCIAL NEEDS SCALE

I wanna do all the things, but not for very long

I'll chill at low-key gatherings

I prefer one-on-one

mostly just messaging

cats allowed, but please, no people

＊still not scientific

Where do you land on that scale? Personally, I've never had much need for socialization, although for many years I tried to convince myself that I *did* like being social. I had a few friends growing up, and I appreciated being invited to things...but when I said yes, I usually found myself regretting it a couple of hours later.

Whenever I went to a sleepover as a child, I was desperately longing for home by 9 p.m. I would huddle in my sleeping bag as everyone else had pillow fights and made prank calls. Even though I was the first one to turn in, I was always the last to fall asleep. It took a long time to calm my frazzled nerves.

During my teen years, my friends wanted to include me, and I worried I'd be missing out if I didn't tag along. I tried to be a good sport as they dragged me to activities like dances and football games.

It was high school; I was supposed to be having fun and making memories, right? But it wasn't much fun, and not all that memorable. I began to make excuses to avoid going out. My friends must have thought my parents were extraordinarily strict, because (according to my excuses) they rarely let me leave the house.

So it shouldn't be much of a surprise that, as an adult, I didn't feel the desire to make friends. I suspect there are other introverts who feel that way, and I think we have some pretty good reasons. Here's a list of just a few of them:

1 We don't need someone else to entertain us. Whether it's listening to music, playing video games, or working on an art project, we know how to have a good time...all by ourselves.

2 Life is demanding. There are only so many hours in a day, and those hours are crammed with errands and obligations. Friendships can be time-consuming!

3 Many of us have pets, and when it comes to friends, pets are the very best kind! (I have two dogs, so I might be a bit biased, but I am also right.)

4 We find most social encounters wearisome. If we spend time with someone who drains our energy, how will we "refuel"?

5 Making friends means meeting new people...and that requires leaving our comfort zone. Finding potential friends can be tricky when we don't want to leave the house.

I rest my case. This concludes Chapter 4.

Wait, not so fast! I'll admit that list was a bit one-sided. It was informed by my previous friendships, which I found more exhausting than fulfilling. That was mainly due to my introversion... but would things be different now that I had a better understanding of my temperament?

Perhaps there was a middle ground between the sort of friendships I used to have and not having any friends at all. Maybe I *could* enjoy having friends, *if* they accepted my introverted ways and respected my need for space.

Assuming I could find some amazing humans like that, would it be worthwhile to cultivate friendships? I was content on my own, so why bother? As I mused over the possibilities, I reached some conclusions about why buddies would be beneficial (yes, even for introverts).

I was sorely tempted to slide another list in here, but I thought my editor would complain, so you're getting a web graphic organizer instead:

So, if you've studied that very informative organizer and decided you might like to have more friends, we first have to figure out where to start. I think it would be best to divide the next few pages into two sections: "Online Friends" and "In-Person Friends."

ONLINE FRIENDS

Let's get one thing straight from the get-go: online friends *are* real friends. I know people (naysayers!) who are dismissive when I talk about my online friends, as though they don't "count." Listen up, naysayers: If there's someone you connect with who supports you, values you, and makes you smile, what do you call that person? A REAL FRIEND.

REAL FRIEND -OR- TACO?

	Friend	Taco
Makes you smile	✓	✓
Comforting	✓	✓
Enjoyable any time of day	✓	✓
Good with lime		✓
Interesting conversations	✓	
Appetizing		✓
Understands your needs	✓	maybe?

To further silence the naysayers, let's make a brief list of why it's so great for introverts to have online friends. What? It's still too soon for another list? Sigh...all right. Let's try something different.

REASONS TO HAVE ONLINE FRIENDS

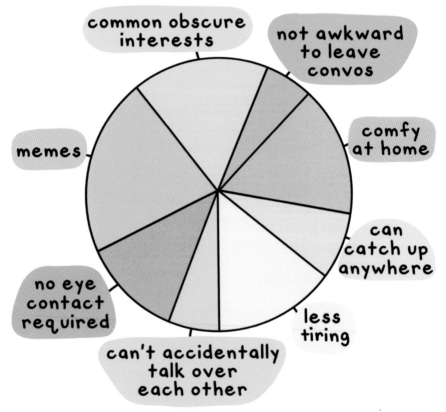

(Now I want pie.)

But where can we find fitting friends on the big wide interwebs? I've managed to connect with some amazing people online in a few different ways. First, I've joined several *Facebook* groups that are very specific to my particular interests. No matter what hobby you have, chances are, there's a group for that!

Secondly, I've made some buddies by playing online games/apps with a chat feature. I like the anonymity of messaging there, plus there are usually filtering and reporting options if someone is being a bad human. There's a game I've been playing for a couple of years now, and I enjoy checking in with the people in my "club."

The third way I've connected with people online is by sharing my creative projects to various forums. I've posted short stories, artwork, and poetry—and offered feedback and encouragement to others sharing their work. Spaces like these can evolve into close-knit communities.

"But Marzi," says my doting mother, "is it safe to make friends online? How can you be certain who you're talking to, Green Bean?"

It's true that I can't be certain who I'm talking to, but I don't consider that a problem. I don't need to know about somebody's appearance, location, or real name to enjoy hanging out with them online. In fact, it's pretty cool to be free from the arbitrary categories that deter people from forming friendships. (And don't worry, Mom: I don't confide personal info, send money, or share my account passwords online. I haven't fallen for a "wealthy single near me" either.)

Now let's move on to the second section: making "in-person" friends.

IN-PERSON FRIENDS

Here's where things get a bit sticky. How are we supposed to make friends when we'd rather not leave the house? The good news is, you don't have to step *too* far out of your comfort zone. You don't have to go to a party or karaoke bar if that isn't your thing; you'll probably have a better chance of meeting like-minded folks if you're doing something you enjoy.

I'm going to share a few strategies that can help you find people you click with. Spoiler alert: The common theme here is *be yourself.* "Marzi," you say, "first of all, I hate spoilers. Second of all, that is the most overused piece of advice ever."

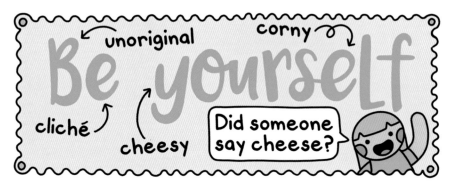

I agree: Spoilers are terrible, and that is indeed a trite suggestion. But it's true! You won't find "your people" by pretending to be someone else.

Weird & Wonderful

All of the following suggestions focus on ways to show others who you are…without having to act like you're an extrovert. Let your quirks show, let your weird flag fly, and the right people will be drawn to you. Here are three ways to find "your people."

Wear items that reflect your interests/identity. As introverts, we might "play it safe" with our clothing so we can blend into the background. We typically don't want attention, but if your goal is to meet someone new, clothing can provide helpful clues about your interests and personality—before you even say a word.

MY "CLUE" CLOTHING

You could put on a T-shirt that references your favorite movie, or perhaps wear a piece of jewelry you crafted yourself. Maybe you could sew a cat patch onto your bag, or add a pin of a cartoon character you love. You could rock a pair of rainbow shoelaces, or a hat with the logo of your favorite sports team. People might strike up a conversation if they care about the same things.

Chatting with strangers can be awkward, but this is different from the small talk introverts hate so much. Instead, you've found common ground with a potential friend, and that leads to engaging conversations about things you love.

Practice your hobby in public. Again, this can feel a bit weird at first. I think most introverts would prefer to do those activities in the privacy of their own homes. But bringing your hobby along is a low-key way to meet people who are interested in similar things. Knit on the bus, read in the park, or doodle in your favorite coffee shop.

Here's the catch: Don't wear your headphones. (Wow, you just groaned so loudly I could hear you from here!) As every introvert knows, headphones are the universal sign for "leave me alone"—but that isn't the vibe you want to send if you're hoping to make a new buddy.

Often when I bring my iPad along to work on digital art, someone will stop to ask me a question about what I'm doing. That often evolves into a conversation about comics, drawing, or our favorite artists. This is a relatively painless way to meet new people, since they approach me instead of the other way around.

Engage in activities you're passionate about. Even though I'm super introverted, I'll step outside of my bubble to get involved with causes I'm passionate about. I care deeply about improving access to mental health resources within my community, so I've attended related seminars and conferences, earned certifications, and served with a Suicide Prevention Coalition.

All of those activities pushed me beyond my introvert comfort zone, but they were worthwhile because they were for causes I care about. Those experiences led me to people who were also passionate about mental health, and we formed bonds of friendship as we worked toward a common goal.

Of course, the activities you engage in don't have to be limited to volunteer work. Do whatever you enjoy! Consider joining a book club, a sports team, or enrolling in a community class. When you pursue something you're excited about, it becomes much easier to find people you can relate to.

Finally, a caveat: Listen to your body and take breaks as needed. A little stretching is healthy, but pushing beyond your limits is not. Remember, forming friendships can take time, and that's okay.

If one of those methods worked for you (congrats!), there are still a few details to figure out. When I first made friends as an adult, I found myself falling into the same old patterns I did when I was younger: I didn't want them to think badly of me; I wanted to be a good sport; I worried that if I didn't go, I would miss out.

When I shared all of this with my therapist, he asked, "So, why don't you tell your friends that?" I suppose I feared—expected—the same rejection I'd experienced in childhood. But, I reasoned, what did I really have to lose? If I didn't explain my introversion—or if they couldn't accept it—then my friendships would remain superficial, and that would be a waste of my limited energy.

So I went for it: I was honest about my needs and preferences. For example, I mentioned how uncomfortable I was with drop-in visits, and that unless they texted beforehand, I probably wouldn't answer the door.

I told them that I appreciated being invited to events, but most of the time I preferred to stay home. "I have a finite amount of 'social points' to spend," I explained.

"A good start, Marzi," said my therapist, "but remember that friendship is a two-way street, and you'll need to expend some effort if you wish to maintain your relationships."

(Hmm, two clichés in one chapter? My editor is giving me the side-eye!) My therapist wasn't wrong, though. With his counsel in mind, I started saying yes to special gatherings more often, and no to events that were less meaningful.

I stopped thinking in terms of "spending" social points, and started thinking in terms of "investing" social points. Yes, my social points were finite, but if I invested them wisely, I could build bonds that would last for years to come.

I realized there are a lot of different ways to be a supportive friend. It's possible for me to make an effort without wearing myself out. For example, I can text my friend a silly photo of my dog when they're having a bad day. I can loan one of my favorite books, lovingly selected just for them. I can listen without judgment, offering unconditional acceptance.

And I can offer to share my string cheese.

Chapter Five | MUSHY STUFF

So, what if you've been thinking that you might like to share more than string cheese with someone? Maybe you're hoping to date and find a partner. Or perhaps you already have a special person in your life, and you'd like to figure out how to balance a relationship with your introverted needs.

Buckle up, because here comes the MUSHY STUFF. What should you look for in a partner? Is it better to date introverts or extroverts? What role does compromise play in healthy relationships? How can you navigate disagreements in a productive way?

Flirting, first dates, and finding love...come along for the ride, because we're going to figure it all out in Chapter 5.

Before we get started, I want to give a shout-out to the folks who are happily mush-free. That is, the people who are single and have zero desire to change their *Facebook* status to "in a relationship." Choosing to skip the love boat ride is a totally valid decision.

Some introverts avoid romance because they enjoy having more personal freedom and space. Others might be aromantic, and simply have no interest in mushy stuff. And most introverts know that they don't need someone to be their "other half" in order to be "whole."

Whatever your reasons, I would never try to convince you that a partnership is a prerequisite for happiness. If you've decided that you're a lone wolf and wish to fly solo (that's a terrible mixed metaphor; let's see if my editor will let me keep it), you might wish to skip forward a few pages to the "Compromise" section within this chapter, as it can be relevant to all types of relationships.

lone wolf flying solo

Assuming that you aren't a flying wolf, I think the best way to start your mushy journey is with—you guessed it—a LIST. But this time, *you're* going to be the one writing the list.

Before you delve into flirting, dating, and finding love, it's a good idea to think about what you're looking for in a partner. Creating a list like this can help clarify what's important to you, which will make it easier to spot potential partners when they come along.

LIST TIME

You're free to put whatever you'd like on your list, but I'd suggest focusing on the values and traits that are most meaningful to you.

It's a good idea to keep the items on your list general rather than specific. For example, you might write "a hard worker" rather than "a wealthy doctor who is also a ferryboat captain."

"But Marzi," you say, "Why on earth would anyone put *that* on their list?" To which I say, "I don't know; it was just an example! I've certainly never imagined sailing into the sunset with rich Dr. Captain, MD. Can we just move on, please?"

Moving on: My point is, you're severely limiting the pool of potential partners if you restrict your search to narrow parameters. Remember to keep your list realistic. No one is perfect, and if you're waiting for perfection you'll be waiting for a very long time!

Okay, I know I said that *you* would be writing the list, and hopefully you've already started. But I love list-making so very much…you'll let me join in on the fun, right? I present: my potential partner list(s).

{Unreasonable}	{Reasonable}
☐ owns a skyscraper	☐ kind to animals
☐ double-jointed	☐ doesn't mind silence
☐ likes pineapple on pizza	☐ has a gentle soul
☐ fluent in Klingon	☐ a creative thinker
☐ excellent square dancer	☐ respects boundaries
☐ hates crinkle-cut fries (waffle fries preferred)	☐ enjoys learning
☐ has beautiful penmanship	☐ makes me laugh
☐ can juggle eggs	☐ my dog approves of them
☐ drives a hover car	☐ tries hard
☐ takes care of rescued koalas	☐ is patient
	☐ loves books

As you're making your "potential partner" list, you might be wondering something I'm often asked about. "Marzi," you say, "I am taking this list-writing exercise *very* seriously and I have a pressing question. Should I add 'must be introverted' to my list?"

"Should I only date introverts?"
This question is...

A very good question, my friend. Well, there are some obvious perks to dating another introvert. They're generally okay with low-key activities and breaks between social outings. Introverted partners appreciate quiet evenings and understand the need for personal space. Plus, there's a good chance that they'll be okay with lengthy text threads rather than long phone calls.

Many introverts have a calming presence that feels like a refuge to their partners. So clearly, you should only date introverts...right?

Not necessarily. There are also advantages to dating extroverts. It can be nice to have someone else be "the outgoing one" who handles conversations with ease. Extroverted partners can introduce introverts to new activities they might not try on their own. Plus, they can add a bit of excitement to the relationship. Extroverts and introverts can balance each other out, each bringing their own strengths to the table.

TLDR: You might be missing out if you reject someone solely because they're an extrovert. When determining whether to date someone, perhaps a more important factor is to consider what sort of "energy" they have.

As introverts know, some people have a more "draining energy" than others. If you find someone's energy refreshing, they might be a good match—whether they're introverted or extroverted.

Now that you have a good idea of what you'd like in a love interest, it's time to figure out where to find potential partners. Oh, wait! We already covered how to meet new friends in Chapter 4! Conveniently, all of that advice applies to finding a person you might be romantically interested in. So, if you could use a recap, flip on back; otherwise, we're going to move on to the fun stuff: flirting and dating.

"Marzi," you say, "when you say 'fun stuff,' do you actually mean 'excruciatingly awkward torture'?" Ah, I should have known you were too smart to fall for my peppy phrasing. Yes, I do agree that flirting and dating can be extraordinarily awkward for introverts. Perhaps we could minimize some of the awkwardness with some basic dos and don'ts of flirting.

DON'T	DO
Send anonymous love letters (they're creepy).	Be chill. "Liking" their Instagram posts from 5 years ago isn't a good look.
Rely on cheesy pick-up lines. Everyone loves cheese but no one likes cringe.	Give genuine compliments. Bonus points if they're about something other than their appearance.
Laugh at everything they say. Nobody is that funny.	Ask thoughtful questions. Many people like talking about themselves.

That's a good start! But I think you might find it relevant if I confess a few of the specific missteps I've made while trying to flirt. I'm sure you'll enjoy laughing at—er, learning from them.

I've made all of the missteps...

so you don't have to!

Mistake number one: prioritizing being agreeable over being authentic. I backed myself into a corner once while trying to hit it off with someone. He was talking so quickly that I didn't have time to formulate replies that reflected my own views, so I just found myself agreeing with everything he said. At one point he mentioned how much he enjoyed following NHL hockey.

Oh yeah, hockey is awesome.

You like hockey, too? Who's your favorite team?

PANIC

So there I was, looking pretty ridiculous because even though I thought hockey was "awesome," I couldn't name a single NHL team. At that moment, I really wished for a pillow to tuck my head under!

As introverts, we often expend a lot of energy trying to keep up our end of the conversation. We might be considering someone's statement, formulating an opinion about it, and preparing to share our thoughts—only to realize that the conversation has already moved on to another topic.

If you find yourself feeling flustered mid-convo, you might try this technique I picked up from years of working with therapists: Ask, "How did that make you feel?" Kidding! Kind of. In a more general sense, the idea is to engage in active listening: paraphrasing what the speaker says, then asking open-ended questions that encourage them to elaborate further.

For example, instead of pretending to like hockey and subsequently wanting to crawl into a hole (along with my pillow), I could have said something like, "It sounds like you're a big fan. I don't know much about hockey; tell me what you like most about it." Authenticity intact, and awkwardness avoided!

Mistake number two: engaging in total avoidance. I can remember having a crush on someone in high school...the more intensely I grew to like him, the more I avoided him. I learned his class schedule—not to "accidentally" bump into him, but to avoid bumping into him. I wanted him to love me, but I also didn't want him to notice me. I'm sure I was sending some mixed signals; I was feeling pretty mixed up myself!

Introverts don't typically like drawing attention to themselves, and that's okay. But, as I've learned, you might seem like a bit of an oddball if you're caught hiding behind a vending machine. There's no need to stalk someone you're interested in (clarification: it is a very *bad* idea to stalk them), but be mindful that total avoidance is counterproductive.

Mistake number three: being unaware of my own body language. Once when I was having a flirtatious conversation in a hallway, the other person kept leaning in. A good sign, right? When someone leans in, it means they're interested in what you're saying (and perhaps in you personally). I would take a tiny step back every time he leaned in; I didn't even notice I was doing it. But he did. He laughed and said, "Where are you going?"

Me subconsciously moonwalking away from conversations...

Like most introverts, I wanted to maintain my "bubble" of space. There are additional body language behaviors many introverts share: We're uncomfortable with extended eye contact (so intense!) and might choose to look anywhere but at the person we're speaking to. We are also reserved by nature, and that might manifest as a neutral facial expression.

There's nothing wrong with any of that! But it's helpful to be aware that our body language is providing cues to others. Showing interest may be as simple as tilting your head and occasionally nodding while they speak; it demonstrates engagement even if you aren't talking. Paying attention to nonverbal communication can take some practice, but it's an especially useful skill for us quiet folk.

NONVERBAL COMMUNICATION as demonstrated by Kiko

head tilt

wagging

lil' smile

"Marzi," you say, "your expert advice worked, and I am in a relationship with an exemplary human. Now what?" Do you remember the Introvert Social Needs Scale in Chapter 4? I think it's key for couples to discuss what they need in terms of interpersonal socialization within their relationship, and what they need in terms of alone time.

Movies portray happy couples doing everything together. They love each other *so much* that they can hardly bear to be apart for even a *single day.* Despite what the media tells you, it's all right for your relationship to look different. I'm going to doodle a few diagrams to show some variations of the Togetherness Model.

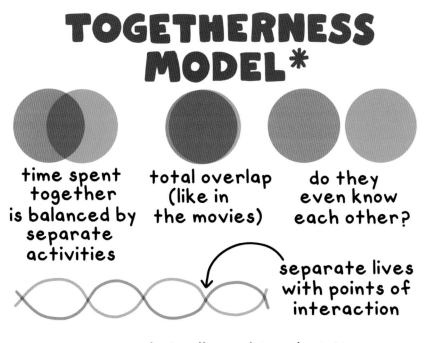

TOGETHERNESS MODEL*

time spent together is balanced by separate activities

total overlap (like in the movies)

do they even know each other?

separate lives with points of interaction

*not technically a thing, but it sounded academic, so I'm going with it

Understanding each other's expectations can mitigate some misunderstandings before they occur. "But Marzi," you say, "what if we each prefer a different version of the (very official) Togetherness Model?" Ah. That leads us to a very important section:

COMPROMISE

If you skipped to this section from the beginning of the chapter, welcome back! I missed you terribly. You've arrived just in time for a public service announcement!

PSA: There is a difference between *needs* and *preferences.* Your needs and preferences may not always remain constant. For example, some days you might *need* to be alone for your own well-being, whereas other days you might *prefer* to be alone but will be okay if you aren't.

When you have a need, by all means do your best to fulfill it. But when it comes to preferences, there's a little wiggle room for compromise.

Okay, now, where were we? Oh, yes, we were discussing what to do when two people have different preferences in terms of togetherness versus space. Maybe I've already spoiled it (I know, I know, you hate spoilers), but I was going to suggest that there may be room for compromise. For example, being in the same room but doing individual activities might be enough to satisfy one person's desire for togetherness, as well as the other person's wish for solitude. Or it might work to block out a few hours for prescheduled alone time.

There may also need to be some compromise when it comes to the type of activities you do together—I've learned that lesson the hard way! One time an extroverted boyfriend invited me to an all-day party at a lake house with a dozen people. There would be dancing, boating, and jet skiing. I said yes to make him happy, even though it didn't seem like something I'd enjoy.

Dancing + boating + jet skiing + people...

What could go wrong?

I was right. Too many people, too much noise, and too much action for an introvert! I tried to be a good sport, but it eventually became too overwhelming. I ducked into a bedroom until my boyfriend tracked me down and asked what I was doing. "Hiding," I said sheepishly.

What are you doing?

Shh! Don't give away my hiding spot!

When I was invited, I wish I'd had the courage to say, "I won't be able to spend the whole day there, but I'd enjoy boating with you for a couple of hours. I can drive my own car so you can stay as long as you'd like. Would that work for you?"

Proposing compromises can feel uncomfortable at first, especially if you are eager to please someone. But when we approach relationships with an all-or-nothing attitude, that means that someone will end up with "nothing," and that does not bode well for a healthy relationship.

"But Marzi," you say, "what if we disagree and reaching a compromise isn't that simple?" Luckily for you, I've had plenty of disagreements, so I can share some insight on how introverts can handle conflict and communicate more effectively.

Do you remember when we talked about the unique strengths of introverts in Chapter 1? There's one introvert skill that comes in handy during disagreements: We're great listeners. I like to give the other person a chance to fully explain their point of view before sharing my own. Sometimes just allowing the other person to vent with minimal interruption is enough to diffuse some tension.

When it's my turn to speak, it often takes time for me to pinpoint what I'm feeling, and even longer for me to decide the best way to communicate it. Sometimes I'll even play out entire conversations in my head!

ENTIRE CONVERSATIONS IN MY HEAD

"I DON'T WANT TO PET YOUR DOG."

But everyone loves Kiko!

Are you a monster?

"Eh, she isn't all that great."

"I'm just scared of dogs."

"Yes, but my hands are covered in honey, I cannot pat."

"I'm a Gorgon, didn't the snakes give it away?"

If the other person is standing there waiting, they might get the impression that I'm ignoring them. I've found it helpful to explain, "I hear what you're saying, and I'm taking a minute to think it over." This shows that what they've said is important to me, and it's worth my time and consideration.

If things do begin to escalate and we're becoming more upset, I start to feel overwhelmed. Like most introverts, I need to take short breaks when overstimulated. Stepping away from a disagreement for a while isn't a bad idea; it gives us both time to replay the conversation and refocus on the purpose of the discussion. It's important to give the other person a heads-up: "I'm not walking away from this; I just need a short timeout to calm down. I'll be back in five minutes and we can talk about it further." Usually we both return feeling calmer and more clearheaded.

FIVE-MINUTE TIMEOUT

Replay & refocus.

Sometimes we reach a compromise after talking through things. Sometimes it doesn't work out that way. When it's clear that we just view things differently, I try to wrap up the discussion by rephrasing what they've expressed to show that I've heard and understood how they're feeling. I like to remind myself that I can validate their feelings even if I don't agree with their point of view.

Your feelings are valid.
(Even though you're wrong.)
Uh-oh, did I say that last part out loud?

"But Marzi," you say, "how do I know if it's worth maintaining a relationship with someone, or if I should cut ties and move on?"

I hope you don't return this guidebook if I admit I don't know. I can't tell you whether you should keep a certain someone in your life (unless it's a dog, then the answer is yes, definitely keep them in your life).

Remember the earlier exercise where you made a list of traits you'd like in a partner? It's also wise to make a deal-breaker list. This is a list of red flags that are signs of an unhealthy relationship. Here are a few things you might consider adding to your deal-breaker list:

DEAL BREAKERS

- They resent my independent activities.
- They display passive-aggressive behavior.
- They disrespect my boundaries.
- They refuse to consider compromise.
- They act jealous or possessive.
- There's too much drama and not enough joy.
- They are abusive in any way.

Whether you're riding the love boat or whether you're a lone wolf flying solo, you deserve respect. Remember that you are a whole, beautiful human, all on your own. Healthy relationships can be fulfilling, but remember that you don't need anyone else to complete you...not even rich Dr. Captain, MD.

Chapter Six | PUBLIC RELATIONS

In the previous two chapters, we talked about how introverts can find people they actually want to connect with. But what about those occasions when you'd prefer not to connect with anyone, but you need to venture out anyway?

Like most introverts, there are few places I'd rather be than inside my cozy little home. Sometimes I feel somewhat (read: completely) frazzled when I have to navigate the world beyond my front door. Unfortunately, even introverts must make the occasional public appearance.

In this chapter, we'll talk about how to cope in crowded places and deal with large-scale events. From traveling to weddings, we'll figure out how to find our way in a world full of people. When we have to "go public," it pays to be prepared!

If I were to describe my decorating style in one word, it would be "introverted." A sign above my fireplace reads, "It's so good to be home," while a throw pillow on my couch says, "This is my happy place." A wood plaque on my bookshelf suggests, "Let's stay home," and a cross-stitch by my front door states, "An introvert lives here. Please don't overstay your welcome." (I stitched that one myself!)

As with a lot of introverts, home is my favorite place on earth. I'm surrounded by the things I love most: books, houseplants, quilts, and snacks.

Needless to say, I'm not very keen on leaving my cozy nest to deal with crowded public places. But like it or not, sometimes it's inevitable.

Take, for example, shopping. It's become simpler these days now that many places offer online ordering (plus delivery right to your doorstep). But what if, heaven forbid, we have to actually go *inside* a store?

MAGICALLY APPEARING GROCERIES

There's a certain business that won't ship many items to my zip code (including pillows, which seems particularly strange, but the workings of this store are cloaked in mystery).

"But Marzi," you say, "why not just reveal the name of this mysterious store?" Well, my ever-curious friend, my editor would probably cross it out 'cause legal reasons. Besides, if I told you, it would ruin the mystery!

Cloaked in mystery!

NAME REDACTED

Anyway, I braved the four-hour drive to pick up some Ostkudder and Delfinplattor (or something like that). It was nice at first, wandering about and looking at things I never knew I needed. But gradually the lights seemed to grow brighter and the crowds larger.

Why were there so many people there at once? Could there really be such a high demand for Potatisgaffel?

Ostkudder

Delfinplattor

As a migraine descended, I fumbled in my bag for aspirin and sunglasses. Did I look silly wearing sunglasses in a store with no windows? Probably. Did I feel better once I put them on? Definitely.

Shopping while fabulous!

And more importantly, while comfortable.

These days, I won't even go into a grocery store unless I have my sunglasses and headphones with me. I've decided I care more about how comfortable I am than how I look in public.

I also find it helpful to have a shopping list handy on my phone, organized by aisle. I'll try anything that minimizes my time in a busy store!

SHOPPING LIST

PRODUCE
Kiwis
Radishes
Artichokes

DAIRY
String cheese
Feta
Blue cheese
~~san~~

CANNED
Alphabet soup
Cream corn

BAKING
Cupcake liners
Sprinkles
Cocoa

Don't forget the dog treats!

Another inevitable public venture: traveling. I know there are some introverts who love to travel, and if you're one of them, I'm rather envious. I always get terribly homesick, and I've always been an anxious traveler.

I once had to go on a business-related trip and flew into the San Francisco airport. That was all right, until I had to *depart* from that airport. The security lines were much longer than I had expected, and it was all very loud. It didn't take long for me to become disoriented.

Eventually I found my terminal and settled down to wait. When they announced that it was time to board, I got in line...only to be told that I had the wrong gate, and this flight was not headed home, but to Canada! Oops!

"But Marzi," you say, "how could you possibly have—" Hey, it isn't my fault that some international flights share Terminal 3! Anyway, that isn't the point. The point is, crowded, noisy airports can be overwhelming for some introverts.

After that fateful trip, I resolved never to fly anywhere again. But then I thought about how terrible it would be to sit next to a stranger for a twelve-hour bus ride, and I rethought my strategy. Instead, I made some basic but beneficial adjustments to my travel routine.

This is Chapter 6, a *new chapter*, and that means NEW LISTS!
Let's kick things off with this one:

TOP FIVE TIPS FOR SURVIVING AIRPORTS

1 Search for a map of the airport online. Take a look at where you'll check in, how to find your gate, and where you can buy a giant cinnamon roll. It's a lot easier than wandering aimlessly through bustling crowds (and possibly ending up in Canada).

ACTUAL* AIRPORT MAP

my gate

or maybe this is my gate?

TERMINAL 3

cinnamon rolls

*more or less

2 Arrive early. "But Marzi," you say, "why would I want to spend any more time at an airport than I have to?" Because there's nothing worse than being late, stressed, *and* overstimulated at the same time. You might find it preferable to deal with the lines, locate your gate, and then relax in a quiet corner chair. You can wind down and charge your phone while listening to your favorite playlist.

3 I suggest bringing a hoodie. Not only is it the cozy-comfy uniform of introverts everywhere, but it also doubles as a portable hideaway. It provides a bit of privacy and helps block out bright lights, people, and noise.

4 Remember that this experience is temporary. You can get through it! Within several hours, you'll arrive at your destination and can sprawl out on a big, soft bed.

5 Buy the giant cinnamon roll. You deserve it.

As long as we're talking about travel, we should also discuss vacations. Depending on the circumstances, vacations can either be rejuvenating or stressful for introverts. After being on (more than) a few miserable vacations, I have some suggestions to ensure your vacation is a more positive experience.

Protect your energy. Raise your hand if your level of enjoyment varies depending on who you're vacationing *with.* In Chapter 5 we discussed how a person's energy affects how quickly an introvert feels drained. Vacationing with others can be exciting, but remember to frequently check in with yourself. Are you maintaining your mental and emotional equilibrium? Practice self-care to protect your energy.

Insist on flexibility. Introverts don't always know when they'll begin to feel burned out. It doesn't matter how much others cajole or complain; no amount of convincing will make you feel better. The only cure is downtime, so make sure your travel plans are flexible.

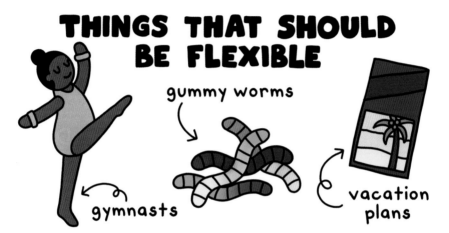

THINGS THAT SHOULD BE FLEXIBLE

gummy worms

gymnasts

vacation plans

You don't need to spend every minute with your companions. On a trip to Las Vegas, I wanted to relax by the pool but my partner wanted to watch a sports game. I was irritated until I realized: *We don't have to do everything together.* As long as you're visiting a safe location, it's okay to split up to pursue your own interests.

See you in a few hours.

Have fun!

Prioritize while planning. There may be a million fun things to see and do, but it's impossible to do them *all*. It's a good idea to plan ahead and make a prioritized list of what you're looking forward to. Maybe you won't get to cross everything off the list, but you'll be able to experience the most interesting things.

WHAT WOULD YOU LIKE TO DO?

visit a museum	go to a concert
rent a cabin	visit an aquarium
go to the beach	relax at a coffee shop
ride on a ferry boat	see a landmark
visit a historical site	go on a hike
go to a festival	buy souvenirs
see a show	go snorkeling
swim in a pool	sleep in every day
browse book stores	visit a zoo
eat local cuisine	take scenic photos

Don't feel guilty for indulging in activities you could do at home. You might feel pressured to spend every minute visiting local sites. But if you want to turn in early and read a book in bed, do it! If you're aching for a long, hot bath, go for it! The entire point of a vacation is to enjoy yourself...so do whatever will bring you satisfaction in that moment.

Take a deep breath, because now we have to move on and discuss the worst-case public scenarios. Yep, I'm talking about the events where headphones and hiding in a hoodie aren't really an option. Take weddings, for example.

Weddings can be particularly painful for introverts. Dressing up and sitting in a crowd of people isn't much fun. It isn't as though you can just stand up and leave in the middle of the ceremony. Plus, weddings can last for *hours.*

The first thing to consider is whether you actually *have* to go. How well do you know the couple? Will they notice or be offended if you don't come? Sometimes couples send out invitations to certain people simply because *they feel they have to*.

Sometimes it's enough to reply to their R.S.V.P. by saying, "Best wishes, but I won't be able to attend." You can show your support by sending a gift, if you're so inclined.

If you must attend, wear the comfiest clothing you can get away with. If seats aren't assigned, look around for someone else who seems introverted. They're probably sitting in a back corner, rather than mingling and chatting.

I suggest asking them if you may sit down, then say something like, "It's nice and peaceful over here." That will reassure them that you won't try to make small talk. If you have to be around people you don't know, you might as well find another quiet person who empathizes with your plight!

I'll admit that I try to duck out of weddings as early as possible. I make sure to sign the guest book, then congratulate the couple and escape as quickly as I can.

Introverts face similar challenges at family reunions. Unfortunately, *everyone* wants to stop and chat there! My strategy is to pull a blitz maneuver. I quickly say "Hello, how are you, what's new?" to each person. After a minute or two of (painful but temporary) small talk, I say, "Oh look, there's so-and-so. I should probably say hello. Please excuse me."

"But Green Bean," you say, "why would you willingly approach everyone there? What kind of introvert are you, anyway?" First of all, never call me "Green Bean" again. Second of all, I know it sounds miserable! But if you get the greetings over with quickly, you can then find a quiet spot to hide without being missed.

WHAT I DO AT REUNIONS

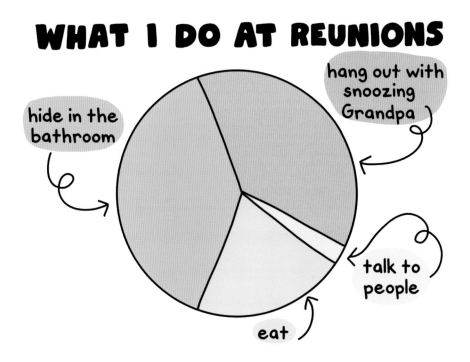

hang out with snoozing Grandpa

hide in the bathroom

talk to people

eat

Funny story: At one family reunion, I found a storage closet that seemed like an ideal place to take cover. I opened the door, only to find another introvert hiding there and texting on her phone! I quickly shut the door and went to find my own secluded spot.

Of course, I always drive my own car to events so I don't have to wait around for others to finish socializing. If it's a gathering with a potluck meal, bring your food in a disposable pan. Then you don't have to hang out until your dish is scraped clean!

For a sensitive introvert, navigating public situations can be a definite challenge. But careful planning and a little preparation makes leaving home a bit easier.

With a few adjustments, some public outings might even be enjoyable...especially if giant cinnamon rolls are involved.

Chapter Seven | WORK HARD

Almost every introvert dreams of working from home. No commute, no dress code, and no one stealing your lunch from the breakroom fridge.

endless fresh coffee

world's comfiest office chair

uniform

delightful coworker

Unfortunately, working from home isn't always an option. In this chapter, we'll talk about employment-related issues introverts face. How do you define a "successful" career? What makes a job "good" or "bad"? Is it possible to be considered a "team player" if you prefer to work solo? From navigating meetings to asking for a raise, we'll figure out how to make work *work*.

We are constantly bombarded with messages telling us what we are *supposed* to want. Traditional media, online ads, posts on social platforms...they all promote a narrative of what success looks like. It's insinuated that the more friends you have, the more important you are. We're also led to believe that your self-worth is linked to a lucrative career. We are taught that you need certain things if you wish to be content.

♡ ◯ ⚇
coolcatz365 If you aren't here, you're a loser 😈

For years, I took most of those messages at face value. I've since realized that I had never stopped to think about what *I* want. What sort of life will bring *me* the most satisfaction? How do *I* define success? What do *I* want in a career?

Those questions led me to reassess my priorities by reflecting on what's important to *me*. Naturally, I made a wish list of things that might bring me satisfaction:

SATISFYING STUFF

a cozy home	a fulfilling career
multiple dogs	plants, plants, plants
books, books, books	time with family
independence	cloning Kiko (maybe)
a reliable car	good mental health
healthy relationships	an indoor trampoline
sharing my doodles	a best friend
being debt-free	learning opportunities
frequent skating	feeling secure
living in a sunny place	swimming with dolphins

Some things on my wish list are conceptual, while others are more tangible. (I'm not entirely sure which category "cloning my dog" falls under.) Unfortunately, quite a few of those things cost money.

We're all familiar with the old adage, "The best things in life are free," but that's one phrase I don't completely agree with.

Maybe some wonderful things in life are free, but a lot of satisfying stuff comes with financial strings attached.

BEST THINGS IN LIFE THAT ARE (NOT ACTUALLY) FREE

Let's be real: We all need some money in the bank account to get by. If we'd like to buy delightful things like cheese fries (*not* crinkle-cut!), then most of us will need a job. (I suppose there are a few lucky people who don't have to work, but alas, I am not in that category.)

delicious, cheesy waffle fries

PEOPLE WHO DON'T NEED TO WORK

lottery winners

princesses

bank robbers

I've taken a nontraditional path (is "professional doodler" an actual career?), but my previous work experience has taught me a thing or two about what helps an introvert thrive in the workplace. And it's also taught me PLENTY about jobs that can make introverts miserable.

I'm going to share some employment experiences I've had, then explain how they measure up on my fancy Employment Suitability Scale.

Let's start with my very first job: calling random phone numbers to conduct surveys.

"But Marzi," you say, "what is *wrong* with you? First of all, why did you think calling strangers would be a suitable job for an introvert? Second of all, only *horrible* humans randomly call people to ask personal questions."

You're right; the questions were terribly invasive. (I can still remember one survey about toilet paper that makes me shudder.)

But as for why I thought it would be a suitable job...you'll recall that I didn't learn about my introverted temperament until later in life. When I was younger, I felt that my preferences were flaws I needed to overcome.

EMPLOYMENT SUITABILITY SCALE

Work is interesting & fulfilling.

Job is fairly pleasant.

Eh, it pays the bills.

Crying during the commute.

Would rather live on the tundra & forage for twigs than go to work.

So I pushed through, despite my discomfort and anxiety. I put up with people yelling at me, swearing at me, and (to my relief) hanging up on me. I had long conversations about granola bars and personal hygiene. (Those were separate conversations, of course.)

The call floor was noisy, with dozens of surveys being conducted simultaneously. There was no privacy whatsoever. I only worked four-hour shifts, but afterward I'd be completely wiped out.

My job as a call center surveyor was definitely at the bottom of my Employment Suitability Scale. It failed to meet an introvert's basic needs: the need for personal space, the need for minimal stimuli, and the need to limit social interaction. That job made life on the tundra seem pretty appealing.

The next miserable job I had was in customer service. "But Marzi," you start to say, and then simply sigh and shake your head. *I needed the money,* okay?

The work ranged from dreadfully dull (helping clients activate their cell phones) to extremely stressful (calming irate customers).

To make matters worse, I had a micromanaging supervisor who liked to hover over my shoulder. There was zero downtime. Ever. In fact, I was once written up for using the restroom too often.

I'll admit that I cried on my way to work (and on the way home from work) more than once. There were several aspects of that job that made it difficult for me as an introvert.

My supervisor insisted that I do everything his way, even when I came up with more efficient solutions. Secondly, the work was boring and there were no opportunities to think creatively...or to think at all, really.

Lastly, there was a great deal of uncomfortable confrontation. It was difficult to stay put while being screamed at, and it was challenging for me to solve problems on the spot. So that work environment wasn't the best fit for an introvert either.

"But Marzi," you say, "are you going to keep complaining about your horrible jobs, or are you going to tell us about one you actually liked?"

Well, I *could* keep complaining, because I have a few more awful jobs I could tell you about. But I think you get the picture: Introverts are unhappy in work environments that are incompatible with their temperament.

So let's move on to a job that would rate "fairly pleasant" on my Employment Suitability Scale. I spent a couple years working as an editor for a small company, correcting and formatting outgoing materials. (Right now my editor is shaking her head, surprised a company would hire someone who takes such pleasure in trite expressions.)

Why did I enjoy that job? I had an office in the basement, two floors down from most of the staff (although the friendly figurines on my desk made excellent coworkers). I could turn on a small lamp instead of sitting under harsh fluorescent lighting. My music played softly on the radio, and when work was slow, I doodled or read.

As an introvert, I valued having my own office space. I liked the freedom of working without much oversight. I enjoyed the soothing, quiet environment I had created to suit my own needs.

Finally, at the top of my Employment Suitability Scale: working from home as a self-employed freelancer. I had a successful DIY *YouTube* channel and website for many years, then transitioned into writing and illustrating.

Yes, there are some trade-offs (the pay isn't great, and, um, TAXES), but pursuing my own interests has been incredibly fulfilling. Like many introverts, I prefer to work independently, and I'm much happier at home than in an office.

Reflecting on your employment history can teach you about what you want (and don't want) in a career. For example, you might select a job that has the option to telecommute, even though it has a lower salary than an office job.

I've come to realize that income is not the only benchmark of a "successful" career. There are other aspects to consider, such as:

Discerning which factors you value most will help you find your way in the search for suitable work.

"But Marzi," you say, "what if I'm stuck in a job that doesn't entail all the factors I value? And what if it isn't practical for me to quit and become a YouTuber?"

It's a hard truth: Sometimes there simply aren't a lot of employment options. Working from home isn't always feasible. That means dealing with coworkers, meetings, and bosses. But there are still ways for introverts to make their jobs more tolerable.

Let's start by discussing something that can be challenging for introverts: establishing positive relationships with coworkers. (I know, working with others wasn't my favorite thing either.)

Many introverts aren't considered "team players" because they prefer to work independently. Unfortunately (and unfairly!), that can potentially have a negative impact on your promotion opportunities. I've come up with several low-stress ideas to help others see you as a valuable asset to their team.

Be a pleasant presence. You don't need to be best buddies with your coworkers, but things will go more smoothly if you try to be pleasant.

I realized I seemed somewhat unfriendly when I didn't acknowledge people existed. I decided it might be worthwhile to put in a little effort. Since I had a hard time remembering names, I kept a notebook where I'd jot them down. I'd also note a few things I learned about that person, like what kind of dog they had or their favorite television series.

I'm not a big fan of small talk, but I've noticed that people feel validated when you mention something that's important to them. (I mean, I know I feel delighted when someone mentions my dog!)

Give credit where it's due. Many jobs are thankless. The daily grind is wearisome, and it's discouraging when no one notices your efforts. Pay attention to what your coworkers have accomplished and express appreciation for their contributions. (If it feels too awkward to do it in person, try leaving a sticky note on their desk.)

Volunteer for tasks you're comfortable with. There are always tasks that don't really fall under anyone's job description, but somebody has to do them. For example, there may be an employee committee trying to plan the annual holiday party.

Although it seems counterintuitive, it's wise to quickly jump in with an offer to do a solo task. Maybe you could create an Evite or pick up a cake from the bakery.

When you volunteer instead of waiting to be asked, you not only demonstrate that you can be a team player, but you're also guaranteed to get the assignment you're best suited to.

Dealing with small committees is one thing, but what's the best way for an introvert to handle long meetings with a large group of coworkers? When everyone simultaneously spews their ideas during a brainstorming session, the chaos can be headache-inducing!

You attempt to consider the ramifications of each suggestion, but the conversation moves too quickly for you to interject (even if you wanted to). Typically, the loudest, most insistent person is the one who ultimately gets the group on board with their plan.

The most *influential* person in the room is not always the most *insightful* (we're looking at YOU, loudmouth Tom), but you don't object because you simply want the meeting to end.

Perhaps your silence in meetings is misconstrued as disengagement (or worse, a sign of limited creativity). So how can you demonstrate that you're capable of contributing original thoughts?

Once you've taken some time to reflect on the meeting, you may wish to send an email to the project manager. You can comment on the most interesting ideas and share observations of the plans presented. Perhaps you can even communicate a few suggestions of your own.

WAYS TO COMMUNICATE AT WORK

NO	YES
charades	emails
Morse code	encouraging notes
writing on bathroom stalls	one-on-one conversations

It's perfectly okay to be quiet most of the time, but it's also important to find methods of conveying your thoughts—they're likely insightful and valuable.

I've saved the scariest aspect of employment for last.

ASKING FOR A RAISE

Yes, your insightful, valuable self may very well deserve a pay raise. While some businesses give raises based solely on length of employment, many others use performance-based models. So how does a reserved introvert convince their employer that their work merits a pay increase?

The first obstacle: You must become comfortable with talking about your skills and accomplishments. "But Marzi," you say, "I don't like talking much, and bragging about myself feels super awkward."

I know it feels a little weird...but you aren't actually boasting. You're simply sharing factual information about your strengths and how you're an asset to the company.

FACTUAL INFO:

You are insightful.	You are an asset.
You are valuable.	You are strong.

If you're having a hard time determining what your forte is, return to the introvert strengths we discussed in Chapter 1. I'm guessing you're an independent thinker with unique ideas. You're probably observant, so you may be attentive to detail. When working alone, you are likely focused and productive. Perhaps you're also self-motivated and don't require micromanaging.

Additionally, you'll want to discuss specific ways you've contributed to the business. Which projects have you successfully completed? In what ways have you gone above and beyond expectations? Do you have an excellent attendance record that proves your reliability? Have you received positive feedback from clients or customers?

Consider writing a brief proposal with a list of your achievements within the company—much like a resume. Seeing your accomplishments in print may help your employer recognize the benefits of retaining you as a happy employee.

Dear Manager,
I appreciate your consideration of my pay raise proposal. Here are a few ways I've made a difference:
• Brought a plate of fine meats and cheeses to the holiday party.
• Reduced my bathroom breaks by 12%.
Restructured Tom's plan to be more efficient.
...ing posters of dolphins

As you find your way at work, it's important to keep sight of why you're there in the first place. Perhaps you have a fulfilling job that ranks high on the Employment Suitability Scale. But even if you don't, working provides a way to afford the necessities of life; you might even be able to buy a few fun things on your Satisfying Stuff wish list. And maybe, if you're truly yearning for it, that salad chopper.

At long last, I have obtained a salad chopper!

Chapter Eight | PLAY HARDER

After a long workweek, we all need the chance to unwind. Isn't it time to have a little fun?

In this chapter, we'll discuss the benefits of making time for play (no, you're not too old!).

We'll talk about some negative beliefs that hold us back from prioritizing playtime. We'll explore some introvert-friendly hobby ideas (have you considered starting a collection?) and find ways to embrace positive free-time activities.

We deserve relaxation, recreation, and rejuvenation. Let's make it happen!

"But Marzi," you say, "is it"—wait just a minute! Are you really going to question my methods before I've even finished the first paragraph? Seriously?! Okay, fine; go ahead.

"But Marzi," you start again, "is it truly necessary to have a whole chapter on playing? We're *grownups*, remember?" Well, yes, I do feel it's necessary (and not because my editor told me so). Somewhere along the way, many grownups forget how important it is to make time for play.

Why don't we make more of an effort to prioritize our interests and hobbies? As adults, it can be hard to give ourselves permission to engage in "non-productive" pursuits. We often feel guilty when we use our free time to focus on fun. We scold ourselves for being lazy when we choose to play instead of catching up on laundry or replying to work emails.

That line of thinking is rooted in the "but we're *grownups*" mindset. We're supposed to be responsible! We're supposed to get things done! We're supposed to have daily to-do lists and cross them off completely!

Why should you make time for play when there are other important tasks to complete? I think there are several answers to that question.

1   Playtime reduces stress. It gives you a much-needed break from the demands of adulting. Playing steers an introvert's busy, overthinking brain in a refreshing new direction.

2. Some forms of play help introverts utilize their natural creativity, while other types of fun improve physical health. Engaging in creative activities releases dopamine (the "feel-good" hormone), and exercise releases endorphins (which reduce pain). Our bodies appreciate it when we make time for play!

3. We've discussed how introverts require downtime. Solitary relaxation is not only pleasurable; it also helps you recalibrate. That means you can be more engaged and productive in your other pursuits.

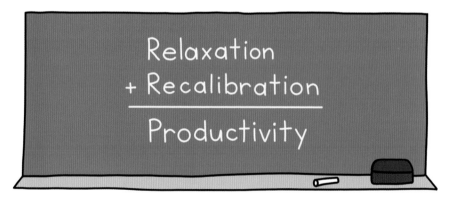

4   Playtime is a wonderful way to reconnect with yourself. Remember how we discussed the importance of nurturing our inner child in Chapter 2? That child needs and deserves attention. Recreational activities help you get in touch with your younger self, and that can be a healing experience.

Before I considered the benefits of play, my insecurities prevented me from embracing activities I now enjoy. I regret how my concerns caused me to miss out on rejuvenating experiences. There were several negative beliefs that held me back; perhaps you've had some of these worries as well?

WORRIES THAT HELD ME BACK

no time

playtime is selfish

my hobbies are weird

I'm nervous to try new things

"But Marzi," you say, "I really *don't* have time to just goof off." I know, life is busy. Between work, family, chores, and errands, it's a challenge to carve out some free time. But it might be worthwhile to wake up a bit earlier (or stay up a little later, if you're a night owl like me) to enjoy some solitary relaxation. (If I'm being completely honest, I'd have a lot more free time if I didn't scroll on my phone so much.)

No new posts. Maybe I should refresh & try again.

When I decided to schedule in some fun, I noticed my anxiety levels were reduced. When I felt overwhelmed or stressed, playtime helped me feel more like myself again.

I was also deterred by the belief that playtime was selfish. Wasn't it greedy and thoughtless to focus solely on myself for a while? I now realize that introverts need to carefully balance what they give to others and what they choose to give themselves.

Do you remember the cake doodle in Chapter 3? It illustrated the wisdom of limiting the time you devote to others. While you're giving away slices of cake, it's imperative that you save a slice for yourself. You deserve a fun treat too!

The next worry I had was likely a carryover from my youth: I believed the things I liked were weird, nerdy, and childish. By extension, that meant *I* was weird, nerdy, and childish, and that thought embarrassed me.

In retrospect, that line of reasoning didn't make much sense, because (1) it wasn't as though anyone else would see me playing with squishy toys, and (2) there's nothing wrong with being weird and nerdy or expressing childlike joy.

Once I stopped worrying about how my interests would be perceived, I reconnected with the hobbies I had as a child. I built villages with Legos; I used Play-Doh to create faux cuisine. And it turns out that I still love to create chalk art! I encourage you to rediscover childlike activities to see whether they still bring you pleasure.

As for my weird and nerdy interests...I'm having a lot of fun with those too! I've learned to grow and propagate houseplants (at one point, I owned seventy-five!). I've done fancy photo shoots of my dog. I've added to my extensive book collection, organizing them by category and color. Don't feel embarrassed about whatever hobbies make you happy. You'll live a richer life if you do what you love.

Another thing that held me back from embracing playtime: I was curious about new activities but too nervous to try them. I didn't know where to start, and I was afraid to fail. Why waste my time doing something I might not be good at?

I loved roller skating as a kid, but I hadn't put on skates for more than a decade. When I heard that a local roller derby team was sponsoring a skate camp, I hesitated. I had some fears, including:

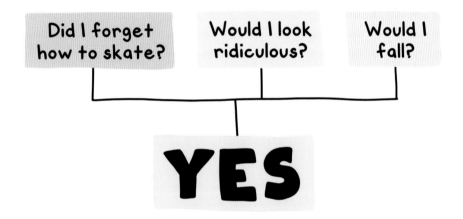

The answer to all of those questions was YES. I could barely stand up on skates. I looked ridiculous when I started to roll and couldn't stop (until I hit a wall). And yes, I fell. I fell again, and again, and again.

But...I was also having fun. I wasn't skilled, but as long as I kept trying, I didn't feel like I was failing. I was *learning.* After skate camp, I decided to continue attending roller derby practice. I was exploring something new, and it felt like playtime!

It was liberating to confront the worries that held me back from embracing play, but there were additional challenges standing between me and activities I wanted to enjoy.

A couple of years ago, my all-time favorite band was having a concert several hours away. I was *so excited* to go that I didn't even think about the impact the crowds, noise, or light show might have on me.

When I arrived, the lines were long and the arena was crowded, but I was so thrilled to be there that I didn't mind very much. At least, not at first. But I only made it through two songs of the opening act before I realized I'd overestimated my ability to deal with that much stimuli.

I left the arena to find a quiet spot in the hallway, but the noise and crowds were just as bad out there. I found my way to an empty stairwell and sat down alone. I felt so upset that I wasn't physically capable of doing something I'd been looking forward to for months.

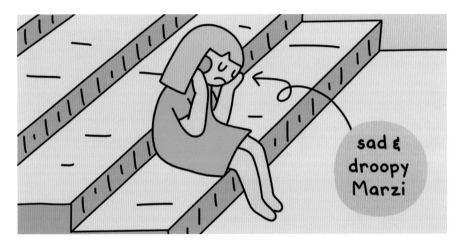

sad &
droopy
Marzi

A while later, a venue employee passed me in the stairwell. She paused and asked if I was okay, and I shook my head and said it was too loud. She asked me to follow her, and led me to a little room where she handed me a pair of complimentary earplugs.

THE HERO
THE WORLD
NEEDS

I was grateful, but I also had mixed feelings. Did I really travel all this way to listen to my favorite band play live, only to muffle it with earplugs? In that moment, I was disappointed with myself for being different, and frustrated that I wasn't able to enjoy events in the same way as my more extroverted friends.

But I decided that wearing earplugs was better than missing the concert altogether. So I put in the earplugs, and you know what? It was fine. It was just right. I could hear well enough without it being too overwhelming.

I also thought I'd miss out on the fun if I didn't watch every minute of the performance. However, I found that I could appreciate the music more if I closed my eyes once the light show and video screen became overstimulating.

I was certainly tired after the concert, but I was also happy. With only minor accommodations, I'd found a way to deal with some introvert challenges that stood between me and free-time fun. (I've since bought earplugs that I could mold for a custom fit, and I even wore them to a Broadway show!)

That leads me to a phrase I've heard multiple times, but still find baffling:

INTROVERTS DON'T KNOW HOW TO HAVE FUN.

Introverts know what a *ridiculous* statement that is. Introverts may need a few accommodations or the occasional break, but *of course* we know how to have fun! It's just that an introvert's idea of fun may be different from an extrovert's concept of fun—and that's okay.

Extroverts tend to enjoy themselves more when they're hanging out with other people, but that isn't true for introverts. Case in point: I don't remember a single person at the most enjoyable event I ever attended...but I do remember a lot of dogs!

One of the best days of my life was spent at Corgi Con—which is exactly what it sounds like. Hundreds of corgis congregated on the beach to frolic in the sand and surf. I got to pet all the dogs I wanted that day. It was pure playtime!

Since introverts instinctively know how to have fun by themselves, they're often drawn to solitary hobbies. I know introverts who spend their free time gardening, reading, cycling, and painting.

If you're looking for new ways to have some solo fun, you might consider one of these introvert-approved activities:

building models

hiking

sewing

playing music

cooking

taking photos

yoga

collecting

Personally, I love outdoor skating. I like the feeling of sunshine on my shoulders, the wind in my hair, and wheels on my feet. Best of all, it's an activity I can do all by myself!

Of course, playtime doesn't have to be a concrete, hands-on activity. For example, your idea of fun might be relaxing outside and enjoying the weather.

Or maybe you like to spend your free time listening to music or daydreaming.

There isn't really one "right way" to have fun. Playtime is simply engaging in whatever activity makes you feel rejuvenated. Spend your free time in the way that makes you happiest— whatever that may be!

HOW SHOULD I SPEND MY FREE TIME?

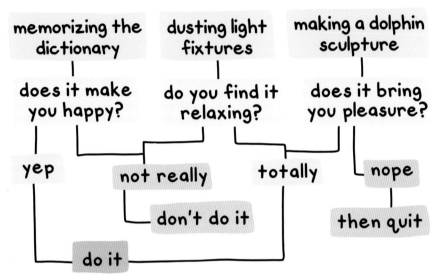

memorizing the dictionary → does it make you happy? → yep / not really

dusting light fixtures → do you find it relaxing? → not really / totally

making a dolphin sculpture → does it bring you pleasure? → totally / nope

not really → don't do it

yep + totally → do it

nope → then quit

Give yourself permission to invest in playtime and have a little fun. Enjoy the many benefits that playing has to offer...and don't forget to have a slice of that cake!

MENTAL HEALTH MATTERS

Embracing playtime is a key way to improve your overall well-being. But it's only a small piece of a bigger picture; our quality of life is linked to many other aspects of mental health.

In this chapter, we'll have a heart-to-heart chat about thought patterns, toxic positivity, and therapy. I'll share self-care ideas and coping techniques that have helped me along the way. (Kiko would like to point out that she has also been helpful along the way. Should we let her contribute to this chapter too?)

Let's take the time to delve into these topics, because mental health matters!

Why did I include a chapter on mental health in a book about introverts? It's because introverts sometimes feel out of place in a world full of people. We can be out of sync with social expectations, and there are constant demands on our time and energy.

Trying to find our way when we're "running on empty" can leave us feeling depleted and discouraged. However, prioritizing our mental health can boost our sense of security and stability, empowering us to approach the world on our own terms.

I'm passionate about mental health advocacy because I've had my own challenges in that domain. Although I'm not a mental health professional, I feel I've had enough personal experience (and therapy!) to offer a bit of introverted insight on the subject.

When we covered the topic of introvert attributes in Chapter 1, we talked about how introverts like to think...and then think some more! It's a wonderful gift, but sometimes it can be hard to rein in our thoughts when they take a negative turn.

Over the years, I've acquired a (terribly impressive!) collection of negative thought patterns. Those harmful ways of thinking distort my perception of the world, while significantly impacting my mental health. To make matters worse, they have a way of becoming self-fulfilling prophecies.

I've devised four strategies to help amend unwanted thought patterns. (I've named those strategies so they all start with "re," because isn't that catchy?)

Recognize toxic phrases. I'm talking about the sayings that are so ingrained in your language that you don't stop to consider whether or not they're healthy. Here's one statement I frequently repeated to myself:

"But Marzi," you say, "isn't that an inspirational phrase? What do you have against joy, anyway?" Hey, I like joy as much as the next person! And I do try to cultivate opportunities for joy, like taking time for play. But feeling joy isn't as simple as *choosing* to be joyful.

Choose joy: I'd think those words on difficult days when depression made it hard to get out of bed. Did it help? Not at all. In fact, it did the opposite. Instead of instantly feeling joyful, I immediately felt guilty. If joy was a *choice*, that meant I was *choosing* to be depressed; if I was depressed, it was my own fault.

It wasn't until much later that I realized what a toxic phrase that actually is. "Choose joy" negates a wide range of experiences and emotions. And so it is with many "positive" sayings we don't think twice about:

When we buy into toxic positivity, we are simply masking our true feelings. In the long run, emotional avoidance has a disastrous effect on mental health. Recognizing damaging phrases can help you deflect thoughts that do more harm than good.

Reassess what your brain is telling you. I often get myself in trouble with black-and-white thinking; I view the world in absolutes without seeing the middle ground. My brain tells me, "I *always* get everything wrong" or "I *never* say the right thing."

If you're also inclined to mentally bully yourself, press pause and take a step back. Ask yourself, "Is that really factual? Does it reflect reality?"

I'll admit that when I stop to ask myself if something is actually true, my immediate reply is "YES, IT IS TRUE!" But when I take time to examine my thoughts objectively, I'm able to acknowledge that I don't *always* get everything wrong, and *sometimes* I say the right thing.

Once I've stepped back from the black-and-white thinking, I can reassess the situation in a more logical manner. I can pivot from "I always get everything wrong" to "I made a mistake. That doesn't mean I always make this mistake, and it doesn't mean I'll make this mistake again in the future. It *does* mean that I have an opportunity to learn and try again."

Redirect negative thoughts when they begin to spiral. Creative introverts have powerful imaginations. We can dream up fantasies or conjure up calamities. It's an amazing ability...until it runs amok.

My default mode is believing that the worst possible thing that *can* happen, *will* happen. I am the QUEEN of catastrophic imagination.

When I find myself stuck in an endless loop of catastrophic thought and anxiety, it sometimes helps to follow that line of thinking all the way through to its worst-case conclusion.

FEAR LOOP

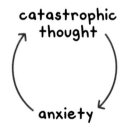

catastrophic thought

anxiety

I remember feeling anxious the first time I went to volunteer at a teen center. I thought, "I'm the most introverted human ever; what am I *doing?* Will the kids even like me? Or will they think I'm uncool and out of touch?!"

So, what if they didn't like me? I decided to follow that thought and imagine the worst that could happen.

I was (pretty) sure they wouldn't beat me up in the bathroom. They might diss me, but I could handle that. And if the kids hated me, there were still other ways I could contribute within the organization.

Redirecting my imagination down a path with a clear ending helped break the catastrophic thought loop. (By the way, a few of the teens thought I was cool. Okay, only two teens thought I was kinda cool. But nobody beat me up in the bathroom!)

"But Marzi," you say, "what if the worst-case scenario actually turns out to be horrible?"

Okay, yes, there are times when that strategy can backfire. For example, I was trying to buy a new house while simultaneously selling my own. I hit a snag when I found a buyer—but my home's appraisal came in lower than expected.

As I followed the path of catastrophic thought, I reached the end and realized, "I might not be able to afford the new house I'm supposed to close on in three weeks!" Um, yeah, that would indeed be a catastrophe. (Spoiler alert: Everything turned out fine.)

When a line of thinking leads to panic rather than clarity, I redirect myself in other ways. I prefer methods I can do in solitude, as I feel most at peace when I'm by myself (can you relate?). I like to deep clean when I'm anxious because I can expel nervous energy in a productive manner. Or I might choose to soak in the bath while listening to a soothing playlist. Both are forms of self-care that help me redirect unhelpful thoughts.

INTROVERT SELF-CARE IDEAS

Hello again, Cheetos chicken cheese casserole!

Cuddle a furry friend.

Watch something that makes you smile.

I volunteer!

Bake something.

To be clear, I'm not advocating for ignoring your problems or the emotions that accompany them. However, redirecting your thoughts by practicing self-care can help you feel calmer and more in control—and that enables you to tackle problems in a more constructive way.

Remember that there are always other perspectives to explore. While introverts like to examine others' ideas, it can be difficult to deconstruct our own thoughts.

I try to analyze my thinking the same way I carefully consider someone else's point of view. I ask myself a list of questions (you know I couldn't write a chapter without a list!):

ANALYTICAL QUESTIONS

Is this line of thinking constructive?

Am I making flawed assumptions?

Is there anything I'm overlooking?

How might someone else perceive this?

Can I approach things in another way?

Remembering that there's more than one way to view a situation—or ourselves—can help you break free of rigid thought patterns while revealing new possibilities.

DIFFERENT PERSPECTIVES

I'm a failure.

You're my favorite.

I'm unlikeable.

I love you.

I'm the worst.

You're the best.

However, if you're having difficulty shifting perspectives, you might consider sharing your thoughts to gain additional insight. "But Marzi," you say, "I am an independent introvert! I don't need someone else to tell me how to think or what to do!"

You're right again, my friend. But what if instead of someone telling you *how* to think, someone listened to *what* you think? What if instead of someone *telling* you what to do, someone offered support while you *considered* what to do?

Luckily for us, there are folks who are skilled at doing exactly that. Licensed counselors, therapists, and psychologists are trained to listen to and validate their clients, which can lead to greater levels of self-awareness and acceptance.

"But Marzi," you say, "I feel like I'm a fairly well-adjusted human. How do I know whether I'd benefit from therapy?" It's my opinion that...

Therapy can help you manage stress, navigate relationships, learn coping skills, and achieve goals. There are many therapeutic styles, and it's worthwhile to research which one would fit you best. You can also choose whether you'd like to have sessions in person, via video conferencing, or by phone. As an introvert, I love being able to have sessions from the comfort of my own home (with Kiko by my side, of course).

When I first started seeing a therapist, I didn't realize that *I was in control of my therapy*. I was working with someone who simply wasn't a good match for me. Our sessions were frustrating and uncomfortable (for both of us, I think). I finally realized that I could decide whether I wanted to continue working with him, or whether I'd like to go somewhere else.

"But Marzi," you say, "how can I tell whether a therapist will be a good fit or not?" There are a few telltale clues I've picked up. Are you in the mood for a list? Because I am!

1. **Mental health professionals should be open to feedback.** If you feel like you aren't being heard or you aren't making progress, it's important to share that information. A good therapist will welcome your input because it leads to more productive sessions.

2 **Mental health professionals must adapt to meet your unique needs.** I had a therapist whose only mode was full speed ahead! He would push too hard when I was at my most fragile. Introverts like to work at their own pace, and a skilled therapist will know how to adjust. To put it in perspective: If you're new to working out, a good trainer won't begin by forcing you to bench-press 250 pounds. Gradual progress is good; pushing to the point of injury is not.

3 **Mental health professionals ought to convey confidence in your ability to grow.** I was seeing a psychiatrist who liked to tell horror stories about others who shared my diagnosis. He'd focus on the worst possible outcomes, which made me believe I was doomed to a terrible fate. Further research taught me there was a lot I could do to mitigate my symptoms. Educating patients about mental illness is important, but it can be framed to emphasize aspects within the patient's control. The majority of your sessions should leave you feeling hopeful, not hopeless.

4 **Mental health professionals will not do the work for you.** Beware of bossy therapists! Competent therapists will point you toward a promising path, not drag you down it. Self-realization is an important aspect of therapy; you should be *discovering* what you'd like to do rather than always being *told* what you ought to do.

It's important to note that even the most experienced mental health professionals can't wave a magic wand and make your problems disappear. Life will always have challenges, but a therapist can help you find your way forward.

WIZARD
magically
fixes
problems

GENIE
magically
creates
problems

THERAPIST
helps you discover
the magic that's been
inside you all along

That is so cheesy.

Oh! Kiko reminded me to mention this: Even if you don't have a therapist, you can still receive (free!) assistance if you're experiencing a mental health crisis. There are hotlines available if you're in immediate need of emotional support—many even offer introvert-friendly messaging options (no phone call required)!

Search online for more info about available resources.

Introverts are often independent, but everyone needs support sometimes— so don't feel embarrassed to ask for help! After all, the phrase "mental health matters" is inseparable from this essential truth: *You* matter.

FINDING YOUR WAY

Chapter 9 covered important information about caring for your mental health. But mental well-being entails much more than the points mentioned in the last few pages. In fact, caring for your mental health encompasses *all* of the ideas we've discussed within this book.

Reflecting on the past, improving your relationships, defining what you want, practicing coping skills—these are all aspects of caring for your mental well-being.

As I've incorporated the positive strategies we've discussed throughout this book, I've grown in self-awareness and self-acceptance.

Let's take a moment to reflect on some of those concepts:

POSITIVE STRATEGIES FOR INTROVERTS

embrace your introversion

nurture your inner child

STOP set healthy boundaries

establish a support network

clarify what is meaningful to you

know when to walk away

find routines that calm you

set your own standards of success

recognize your accomplishments

do more of what brings you joy

remember you're learning, not failing

try something new

practice self-care

How can you find your way in a world full of people? By finding yourself—understanding your needs, recognizing your gifts, and affirming your introverted temperament. Here's to discovering what you value—and what you're worth. Here's to being *Positively Introverted*.

ABOUT THE AUTHOR

Hi! So you want to hear about Marzi, huh? Well, you came to the right dog! I don't mean to brag, but we're kinda best friends. I made a doodle with everything you need to know....

Her favorite cheese is Brie, but she also likes sharp cheddar.

She grows houseplants & likes her Boston fern best (shh, don't tell the others).

Her hobbies include reading, roller skating, and rubbing my tummy.

I've also helped her write a few other books, so check those out, too!

Love, Kiko

More from
bestselling
author

MARZI
WILSON

COLLECT THEM ALL!

Introvert Doodles: An Illustrated Look at Introvert Life in an Extrovert World is Marzi's first book of doodled goodness! From awkward encounters to sweet moments of solitude, this comic collection is an insider's look at the introvert experience.

Pick up or download your copies today!

The Introvert Activity Book: Draw It, Make It, Write It (Because You'd Never Say It Out Loud) is hands-on playtime for introverts! Get out your scissors and markers, because this book is meant to be cut up and colored in! Spark your creativity with art projects, scavenger hunts, list writing, and more.

Pick up your copy today!

adamsmedia
An Imprint of Simon & Schuster
A ViacomCBS COMPANY

In *Kind of Coping: An Illustrated Look at Life with Anxiety*, Marzi gets real about what it's like to navigate life with an anxiety disorder. If you can relate to racing thoughts, nervous habits, and overwhelming worries, you'll find validation—and some useful coping techniques—in this book.

Pick up or download your copies today!

The Little Book of Big Feelings: An Illustrated Exploration of Life's Many Emotions celebrates the wide range of feelings that make us human. Marzi is on a quest to interpret her emotions and discover what they are trying to teach her. She learns to acknowledge anger, understand empathy, and honor hope as she allows herself to feel freely and fully.

Pick up or download your copies today!